Giving the Past a Future

Preserving the Heritage of the UK's Criminal Justice System

Giving the Past a Future

Preserving the Heritage of the UK's Criminal Justice System

Edited by Chris A. Williams

Francis Boutle Publishers

In Memory of John Williams (1944–2004),
who would have been interested

First published by Francis Boutle Publishers
272 Alexandra Park Road
London N22 7BG
Tel/Fax: (020) 8889 7744
Email: heritage@francisboutle.demon.co.uk
www.francisboutle.demon.co.uk

Copyright © Contributors, 2004
All rights reserved.
No part of this book may be reproduced, stored
in a retrieval system, or transmitted, in any form
or by any means, electronic, mechanical
photocopying or otherwise without the prior permission of the publishers.

ISBN 1 903427 21 5

Acknowledgements

This book is the outcome of a conference held at the Open University in June 2004. It is part of an ongoing collective effort concerning the preservation and dissemination of the historical records and artefacts of the UK's criminal justice system. Fifteen years ago, Clive Emsley and Ian Bridgeman set the ball rolling when they first systematically demonstrated the scandalous state of the preservation of most British police records, and since then Clive has continued to keep up the pressure, as has the Police History Society, notably under the leadership of its Patron, Lord Knights.

The event that spurred us into renewed activity was the organisation by the Liverpool University Centre for Archive Studies of a conference in July 2003 on 'Political Pressure and the Archival Record'. Subsequent help from Margaret Procter of LUCAS has been invaluable, and I would urge historians everywhere to follow LUCAS's advice and pay more attention to their raw material, archives.

In developing the themes for the conference, I benefited greatly from conversations with Dave Cross (Police History Society), Louise Connell (Galleries of Justice), and Ray Seal (Metropolitan Police Archive). We were backed by a small grant from the Open University Arts Faculty's Research Committee, and underwritten by the Open University's International Centre for Comparative Criminological Research. The *FBI Law Enforcement Bulletin* and Professor Philip Schertzing (Michigan State University) gave us permission to reproduce copyrighted material for distribution at the conference, for which we are grateful. When getting in touch with the sector as a whole, the *Directory of Police and Crime Museums of the World*, produced by the International Police Association, was invaluable.

The arrangements for the conference and the day itself could not have happened without help, advice, and hard work from Maureen Scollan, Paul Lawrence, Donna Loftus, Stefania Bernini, Peter Claus, Janet Clark, Michael Hassett and (especially and indispensably) Valerie Humphrey. Unlike the papers from many university conferences, which only see the light of day after years or, occasionally, decades, these have come out in a matter of months. For that we have an exceptionally efficient publisher, Clive Boutle, to thank.

Finally I need to thank Dr. Lucy Faire for patience, forbearance, intellectual stimulation, and doing far more than her fair share of childcare during this project.

Contents

9	List of Illustrations	
11	Contributors	
13	Introduction	*Chris A Williams*

Part One: Why Preserve?

23	Chapter 1	A History Worth Preserving? The Unique Policing History of Northern Ireland *Hugh Forrester*
33	Chapter 2	The Metropolitan and City Police Orphanage and the Collective Memory of the Police Community in London *Stefania Bernini*
42	Chapter 3	The Police Vehicle Enthusiasts' Club *Paddy Carpenter*

Part Two: Problems and Pitfalls

57	Chapter 4	British Police Forces' Archiving Policy in 2003 *Chris A Williams* and *Clive Emsley*

65	Chapter 5	History for Sale? The Battle to Preserve Britain's Fire History *Shane Ewen*
73	Chapter 6	A Chance to Find Out *Dave Cross*
81	Chapter 7	Museum Status, Storage Demands and 'Hearts and Minds': Three Insurmountable Areas? *Charles Griffiths*

Part Three: Ways Forward

89	Chapter 8	The Galleries of Justice, Nottingham *Bev Baker*
105	Chapter 9	Essex Police Museum *Martyn Lockwood*
110	Chapter 10	Ripon Museum Trust: Filling the Gap *Ralph Lindley*

Part Four: Institutional Frameworks

121	Chapter 11	The Role of the Museum, Library and Archive Sector *Guy Purdey*
130	Chapter 12	The Effect of Freedom of Information on Records and Archives Management *Kelvin Smith*
138	Chapter 13	Police Force Records Management Policies and the Needs of the Historical Record *Alice Stewart*
151	Appendix	Addresses of Relevant Organisations

List of Illustrations

12   A page from the notebook of PC H.B. Appleton, East Riding Police, 1946
27   The badge of the RIC, as adopted by the RUC in 1922
28   The proposed new crest for the RUC, 1923
30   PSNI crest, from 2001
35   Copy of certificate received on leaving the orphanage, 1907
39   Cover of an information booklet for widows of officers of the Metropolitan and City police forces, published in 1935
40   Leaflet advertising the Annual Concert organised by the Metropolitan Police in 1948
43   Dorset Motor Patrols, c.1935
45   A genuine Somerset & Bath Constabulary Jaguar 340; a replica Bristol Constabulary Wolseley 6/110 Mk II
47   A Ford Zephyr 6 Mk IV 4WD experimental demonstrator, a Rover ex-Met Special Escort Group, a Kent Granada Mk II Srs II and a Hampshire Rover P6 3500
48   Probably the last surviving genuine Hillman Imp panda car
50   A line-up of ex-Sussex vehicles
52   Cars built between 1953 and 1989 greeted HRH Prince Michael of Kent when he opened the Tri-Service Workshops at Gloucester in March 2004
56   Orders for the funeral of Winston Churchill, 1965
78   Poster issued by the Chief Constable of Blackpool in 1932
118   Page from the Surrey Police *Major Incident Handbook*, 1971
150   Letter to the Association of Chief Police Officers from the International Association of Women Police Officers, 1986

Contributors

Bev Baker is the Archivist at the Galleries of Justice: the Museum of Law, in Nottingham.

Stefania Bernini is a Research Fellow in the Open University's European Centre for the Study of Policing. She is currently working on the archives of the Metropolitan and City Police Orphanage.

Paddy Carpenter is the Chair of the Police Vehicle Enthusiasts Club. He is also a member of the Police History Society and a Friend of the Metropolitan Police Museum.

Dave Cross is the Curator of the West Midlands Police Museum in Sparkbrook, Birmingham. He also sits on the Executive of the Police History Society as the Museums Officer.

Clive Emsley is Professor of History at the Open University, and co-Director of the International Centre for Comparative Criminological Research. His many books include *The English Police: a Social and Political History*, and *Gendarmes and the State in Nineteenth-Century Europe*.

Shane Ewen is a Lecturer in Economic and Social History at the University of Edinburgh. He recently completed his thesis at the University of Leicester, on the history of local and national government control over police and fire services.

Contributors

Hugh Forrester is the Curator of the Belfast Police Museum which is operated by the Police Service of Northern Ireland.

Charles Griffiths is the archivist for Dyfed-Powys Police, and has been the Curator of Dyfed-Powys Police Museum for six years.

Ralph Lindley is Honorary Curator of the Ripon Museum Trust, which operates the 'Yorkshire Law and Order Museums' in Ripon.

Martyn Lockwood is Secretary to the Trustees of Essex Police Museum.

Guy Purdey is Head of Standards and Stewardship at the South East Museum, Library and Archive Council.

Kelvin Smith works at the Public Records Office, Kew, for the National Archives. He is the author of *Freedom of Information: A Practical Guide to Implementing the Act* (Facet Publishing: London, 2004).

Alice Stewart is Records Manager for Strathclyde Police.

Chris A. Williams is Lecturer in History at the Open University, and an Associate Member of the OU's International Centre for Comparative Criminological Research.

A page from the notebook of PC H.B. Appleton, East Riding Police, 1946

Introduction

Chris A. Williams

Thirty or so years ago, British historians started trying to write the history of 'the best police in the world'. One of the first things that they noticed is that this institution is incredibly cavalier with the records and historical material needed to secure its place in posterity. Many of the hundreds of police forces that have existed in the UK have left little trace behind them: their records were first merged with those of bigger forces, then destroyed. This has a wider significance than police history (important though that is in itself), because police records are an invaluable resource for the study of all sorts of historical issues.

In 1996, while researching a thesis on policing in Sheffield, I took advantage of a change in personnel at the Sheffield Archives to attempt to look at a restricted file. The book in question was the Conduct and Commendation Book of the Sheffield police, dealing with the period 1831 to 1887. Like all the conduct books in the series, it had been deposited at the archive on condition that it remain closed indefinitely, and I was desperate to see it, both to correlate its contents with the similar records available in Sheffield's Watch Committee Minutes, and to look at the situation before 1843 when the force was 'officially founded'. My request slip was accepted, but the archivist on duty noticed the restriction at the last moment, and, after a tantalising glimpse of a big red volume lying on the trolley, it was wheeled back to the stack, out of my reach. At the time, I cursed the introspection and defensiveness of South Yorkshire Police. However, unlike many of their counterparts, at least they have preserved some archival records relating to their past; many local police forces have been and gone without leaving a single piece of original documentary evidence.

It soon became clear to me that a number of police historians had tried to do something about this situation, notably Professor Clive Emsley, now my colleague in the Open University's International Centre for Comparative Criminological Research. The Centre's police history research group, the European Centre for the Study of Policing, has long been an 'archive of last resort' for unique historical material related to police history. Along with Ian Bridgeman, Clive carried out a survey of the police archives of England and Wales in 1989–90, which was later published by the Police History Society.[1] Yet, as detailed in our account in Chapter Four, police forces have still continued in the main to neglect their past, in spite of the efforts by the PHS and many individuals committed to preserving the records of police forces.

In 2004 we were motivated to hold our conference on 'Preserving Criminal Justice Heritage', largely because we saw that the imminent arrival of the Freedom of Information Act might offer a window of opportunity to finally institutionalise the preservation of police archives. There are other institutions producing records relating to criminal justice, and to an extent this concentration on police forces unbalances the study. However, they constitute a special case for several reasons: the unique power of police forces; the ability of their records to illuminate so much of the world outside the criminal justice system as well as that within it; and above all their status, as neither national nor local bodies and thus the complete masters of their own records. The other issue that we wanted to explore through the conference was the need to set up and secure funding for museums and public collections relating to criminal justice.

Our aim was to concentrate on practical and policy issues in the sector, rather than on academic pronouncements about its significance, valuable though those are in their place. Academics were encouraged to attend and contribute, but as users rather than commentators. Over 80 people attended the conference, including professional and amateur historians from the UK and the Republic of Ireland, museum curators, representatives of local records offices, police administrators and records management officers, and representatives from a variety of national archiving bodies, including the National Archives, the Public Record Office of Northern Ireland, and the Scottish Executive. Producing a short book of the conference papers has allowed us to include material from people who we did not have time to hear from on the day, and for those who made presentations to expand them in written form beyond the quarter of an hour to which they were ruthlessly held. The various chapters, taken together, give a coherent message, first stating the relevance of the sector, then listing some of the challenges which face it, and finally looking at issues that may well shape its development in the future. There are, inevitably, some major gaps in the coverage of the papers, notably regarding the CPS and Customs and Excise, but with luck these will be dealt with in the future.

The first part of the book consists of two essays demonstrating why we need to preserve our criminal justice heritage. Hugh Forrester, of the Police Museum in Belfast, gives an example of a case where police history matters in a very overt way: the legacy and symbolism of the Royal Ulster Constabulary and the Police Service of Northern Ireland. A force which in the past has divided communities, but in the present, in a modified form, has a remit to unite them, has had to re-model its identity. It can adopt a 'white wall' policy in its offices, but, as demonstrated here by the debate about the symbols which it has used, its public face inevitably invokes meanings that are defined by the past. Stefania Bernini shows how the archives of a far less well-known institution – the Metropolitan and City Police Orphanage – can be used to look at many aspects of the way that the Met worked in the nineteenth and early twentieth centuries, as well as at wider issues in social history, such as the changing views of the concept of the orphanage, and of the role of the family in social care.

The second part of the book largely consists of essays examining the problems and pitfalls that face us today. In our chapter, Clive Emsley and myself present the results of a swift – and not especially rigorous – survey that we carried out in 2003 on the archiving policies of British provincial police forces. Our conclusion is that despite a few pockets of excellence, not very much has changed since Lord Knights urged police forces to write archiving policies in the early 1990s. On the other hand, it also reveals a picture of a police service preparing for the arrival of the Freedom of Information Acts. These might carry their own difficulties if access charges are imposed. Shane Ewen has carried out historical research into both the police and the fire service, and his chapter gives an account of the state of research, preservation, and public history in the fire service. He draws attention to an unwelcome development: the new policy for charging for all non-firefighting services could lead to historical research being priced out of the market by charges for access to unique documents.

Dave Cross is the Curator of the West Midlands Police Museum, and what he has learned in this role and in his position in the Police History Society is here used to point to some of the key immediate problems that face those working in museums. Among them are that electronic records are not nearly as durable as paper, that disclosure rules are often confused, and that recent data legislation could have adverse unintended consequences. Charles Griffiths has drawn on his experience as the volunteer curator of Dyfed-Powys Police Museum to give a condensed account of the main problems that must be faced if artefacts and archival material relating to the history of a local police forces are to be preserved. He has also provided a useful guide to the ways that these problems can be overcome. Almost all British police forces have a group of dedicated volunteers who are at some stage of this process: the immense effort required to overcome the 'chicken and egg' problem explains how few have been able to overcome the various obstacles and establish thriving museums.

Had I so chosen, I could have told many stories similar to that of Charles, and included the experience of many police forces whose preservation initiatives are still at this stage in the long hard slog for stability. We have included several different examples of thriving collections in the third section of the book, precisely because collections can thrive in many different ways, but the most common experience in this sector is not success and security. One way to thrive is to remain closely associated with a 'parent' police force. Martin Lockwood of Essex Police Museum charts the experience of one of the most successful of the preservation initiatives in England, deriving from the sustained effort of an active and able group of local volunteers. In Essex, the police museum has forged a very strong working relationship with the Essex Police, who now fund its professional archivist. In an other local 'success story', Ralph Lindley gives details of how the Ripon Museum Trust were able to develop three local sites – a workhouse, police station, and a courthouse – as linked attractions under the label of 'The Yorkshire Law & Order Museums'. Over twenty years of effort has culminated in a recent successful bid for Heritage Lottery Fund money to develop the attraction. The Ripon museums also have an ongoing relationship with the relevant local police forces: notably the North

Riding, but also the West Riding. The documentary records from various forces that survive in the Ripon archive are tantalising, but also frustratingly fragmentary; a condition which is all too common.

Of all the criminal justice museums in the UK, the Galleries of Justice in Nottingham tends to make the biggest impression – not least because of its impressive ability to win prizes. In her chapter, the Archivist at the Galleries, Bev Baker, tells the story of its development and describes its collections. One that stands out is the Rainer Foundation Archive. This spans the whole of the twentieth century, and documents the history of the organisations associated with the London Police Court Mission, the precursor of today's Probation Service. Bev also includes a copy of its acquisitions policy, which is a model of its kind, not least because it notes that we are going to have to start preserving computer software (such as the HOLMES system for major police investigations), if we are to understand the way that twentieth-century criminal justice worked.

The Police Vehicle Enthusiasts Club (PVEC) is another organisation which is committed to preserving artefacts and information which are unlikely to be considered 'historic' by many of those making decisions about whether to keep or discard. As Paddy Carpenter demonstrates in Chapter Ten, the way that cars and vans have been set up and used often gives us an invaluable insight into the way police forces worked. We are unlikely to learn as much about how senior police officers felt about the rank and file from personnel records as we can from noting that, in many cases, forces removed or disabled the existing heaters in their patrol cars, to prevent the occupants from getting too comfortable. From its beginnings as a club for model-makers, PVEC is now carrying into effect its plans for a targeted nationwide preservation plan for historically significant police vehicles. This, as well as PVEC's programmes of systematic research, is as welcome as it might be unexpected to those who assume that a desire to collect is necessarily the product of a purely antiquarian world-view.

The fourth and final part of the collection consists of three papers dealing with the impact of institutional structures on the sector. In his article, Guy Purdey introduces the work of the MLACs – Museums, Libraries and Archives Councils – regional bodies implementing government policy. He sets out a number of areas where they are already helping museums to work better, and draws particular attention to the successful Rural Museums Network as a model which criminal justice museums might want to emulate. The chapter ends with a description of the 'Black Box Project', funded by the South Eastern MLAC, which brought together artists and offenders to create exhibits reflecting on prison. Any rounded consideration of criminal justice has to reflect the concerns and experience of the 'users' as well as the staff. MLACs are not the only public body with a remit to help the sector. Over the last few years, the National Archives have put more effort into acting as an advisory and facilitating body for public sector archivists in general, and one of the fruits of this is their systematic work on the upcoming implementation of the Freedom of Information Act. Much of this has been carried out by Kelvin Smith, and his chapter sets out the structures which public bodies will need to have in place by 1 January 2005 in order to comply with the Act's requirements.

Given the problems regarding police archives revealed in this book, the contribution by Alice Stewart of Strathclyde Police is possibly the most reassuring in the whole collection. It details the way that Strathclyde have set up an integrated records management policy which, by its very nature, leaves a space for assessing the potential historical significance of records once they are no longer useful. Other Scottish forces, in consultation with one another and supported by the Association of Chief Police Officers in Scotland, appear to be following this model. If we could be certain that it is also going to be taken up south of the border then many of our fears about the continuing haemorrhage of records will be assuaged. The attitude taken at the June 2004 conference by representatives of the Association of Chief Police Officers, and of the working group based at Hampshire Constabulary who are writing the FOI guidelines for ACPO, was encouraging.

Participants in the conference seemed to be very pleased with the day, but most saw it as part of an ongoing process rather than an end in itself. Whether or not the implementation of the FOI Act resolves the problem of archiving, it will not solve the problems faced by the sector in delivering historical information to the public, via museums and exhibitions. Securing a future for criminal justice museums is a major piece of unfinished business. Documents – even those selected for easy access for the purposes of family history – are difficult sources which often need interpretation. A museum, on the other hand, can bring the past to the attention of a far wider public than ever read about the topic in books or magazines, however well presented. Its 'public history' function allows it to interpret and present the written and physical record in ways that can (and sometimes even do) reach 'non-traditional' audiences – categories of people who are often thought of in terms of race, but are in fact largely defined by class. In the light of this importance, it is frustrating that the Metropolitan Police Museum, projected since 1948, appears no nearer to materialising. Rightly or wrongly, many people regard the Met as the first modern police institution, yet in this issue it lags far behind our continental neighbours.

The Open University's 2004 conference coincided with the report of the Bichard Committee into the failure of various police forces and other agencies to preserve and collate information that might have led them to spot the Soham murderer, Ian Huntley.[2] While the immediate controversy over the report centred around the power of the Home Secretary to overrule a police authority and suspend a chief constable, its more urgent message was that many or most police forces in England and Wales had given information management a very low priority during the 1990s, and the Home Office – increasingly interventionist though it has become over the last quarter of a century – had not acted to redress that problem. It reminded us that information handling, and thus record management, are among the most important of the police's tasks.

Over the last decade or so, historical researchers have become increasingly convinced that the 'old police' – watchmen and constables – were not the bumbling idiots of repute: instead, they were often highly competent men, an unsurprising fact given that the old police system survived for hundreds of years.[3] But in the first half of the nineteenth century, it was replaced by 'new police' forces, the most famous of which was the Metropolitan Police. As we look into what really changed during this transition, we can see that one of the most important ways in which the new police were distinctive was that they kept a far larger number and variety of records than their predecessors. Not merely records of arrests, but orders, reports of offences, daily reports, suspicions, and the evidence of a host of bureaucratic duties were all crucial in creating and sustaining the structure of authority within these organisations, and defining the format of their activity.

Bichard's conclusions serve as a reminder that the proper handling, collation, and preservation of information is far from being the unnecessary distraction from 'real' police work that politicians of all stripes persist in calling it. Instead, it is one of the most important tasks that any part of the criminal justice system performs: it is what transforms it from a collection of individuals, however well equipped, trained and motivated they may be, into an institution. Individuals retire or perish, but institutions have the capacity to endure, should they so choose.

Notes
1. I. Bridgeman and C. Emsley, *A guide to the archives of the police forces of England and Wales* (Cambridge: Police History Society, 1989).
2. For example, see J.M. Beattie, *Policing and Punishment in London, 1660–1750* (Oxford: Oxford University Press, 2001), and Elaine Reynolds, *Before the Bobbies: the night watch and police reform in Metropolitan London, 1720–1830* (Basingstoke: Macmillan, 1998).
3. *The Bichard Inquiry Report*, HC653 (London: The Stationery Office, 2004).

Part One

Why Preserve?

Chapter One

History Worth Preserving? The Unique Policing History of Northern Ireland

Hugh Forrester

Northern Ireland must be one of the most difficult policing jobs in the world; in a largely divided society afflicted with sectarian strife and which in the last quarter of the twentieth century erupted into what became known as the 'Troubles'. This situation has seen the police caught in the middle where they are often the subject of sustained and brutal attack from both communities particularly during the Protestant 'marching season' of the summer months. This continues even after the various 'cease-fires', and as recently as 12 July 2004, twenty-five officers were injured in a single night of rioting in Belfast.

The model of policing developed in Northern Ireland has had its own symbolism and its archival heritage. The new Police Service of Northern Ireland (PSNI) has inherited a dual role of conventional policing and that of security, inherited from the Royal Ulster Constabulary and before that the old pre-partition Royal Irish Constabulary. As a member of a centralised police force under government control, the policeman in Ireland was often seen, not as a servant of the community, but as an agent of government.

The RUC was born into the turmoil of the partition of Ireland and was faced with a serious attempt to destroy the new Northern state. In such an environment security was paramount and the new Northern government used the Civil Authorities Special Powers Act to combat any terrorist threat, no matter how latent. The Act, renewed annually, then made permanent, gave the Minister for Home Affairs almost unlimited powers to preserve the peace, such as arrest without warrant, internment without trial and the power to ban organisations, meetings and publications. Justification for the act was continued low key IRA activity and a number of limited violent campaigns, such as that on the border between 1956 and 1962. Another key part of the security system was the Ulster Special Constabulary, a part-time armed auxiliary police force which operated in support of the RUC. As its membership was almost exclusively Protestant and Unionist, its existence and use proved contentious with the nationalist community until its disbandment in 1970.

Policing became heavily politicised, not only due to direct control being exercised over the RUC by central government, but also because the force enjoyed a strong association with the prevailing Unionist government. This was particularly the case with senior ranks who enjoyed family and social connections with the political establishment. As a result of its security remit, the RUC continued to be quasi-military in its appearance and equipment, resembling more a British colonial police force than an UK one. The RUC's security training led it, like its forebear the RIC, to offer training courses to colonial officers from throughout the British Empire until the mid-1930s. The military and security aspects of the RUC came to the fore in the ever present sectarian tension, particularly in Belfast, which often led to rioting, such as that following the Jubilee celebrations for George V in 1935. Civil policing developed alongside the security function and the inter-war period saw the foundation of many of the specialisations taken for granted today such as a Fingerprints Branch in 1924 and a Traffic Branch in 1930.

With the rise of the Civil Rights Movement in the late 1960s and the resulting government response, its political control and links with the Unionist government compromised the RUC. Financial constraints imposed on the force by government limited it to a strength of only 3,000, which combined with a lack of resources and equipment meant that it was unable to deal with widespread civil disorder which broke out throughout the Province in August 1969. After major rioting in Belfast and Londonderry, the Unionist government was compelled to seek military assistance in an attempt to restore order. The investigation into the cause of the riots led to a reform of the RUC on the lines proposed by the Hunt Committee, which sought to shape the force into the British Constabulary model while seeking to win the support of the nationalist community. The hopes of Hunt were dashed as the deteriorating security situation in the Province and continued attacks on the security forces turned police stations into fortresses and drove the RUC into reactive security-based policing in many areas. The threat to individual officers and their families, even in their own homes, led to them to retreat from the community at large and to live and socialise together.

A familiar international view of the RUC was of an armed and armoured police force, the necessity for which was seen in the 302 officers killed by terrorist action between 1969 and 2001. Countless thousands were injured physically and mentally. Terrorist cease-fires in the early 1990s led to the 1998 Belfast Agreement which included a reform of policing resulting in the Northern Ireland Police Act of 2000 under which from 4 November 2001 the RUC became the Police Service of Northern Ireland (PSNI). The new service has seen the introduction of many controversial changes; a 'white wall' policy to ensure a neutral working environment and positive discrimination to recruit more officers among the nationalist community, women and those from ethnic minorities. Human rights and equality led training has been introduced for all police and support staff. Organisationally, powers have been delegated to local commanders to enable them to respond more effectively to local policing needs, and they also have civilian advisory support in the shape of local District Policing Partnerships (DPPs). The situation of peace has also allowed a marked reduction in security around police stations and even the opening of new low security stations.

With such radical change in so short a time there is a danger of a rejection of the past by many new officers, who see nothing in common with the RUC past and consciously or unconsciously have adopted a 'year zero' approach, denying everything before the establishment of the PSNI. It will be some time yet before the Police Service of Northern Ireland beds down and is happy with its new identity.

Police symbolism in Northern Ireland

In 1922 the RUC adopted the crest and insignia of the former Royal Irish Constabulary (*see illustration opposite*), including its Harp and Crown badge, granted to it by the Crown for its part in the suppression of the Fenian Rising in 1867. The Harp has traditionally been used by both traditions in Northern Ireland, though whether the harp is alone or subservient to the Crown has been an important symbolic distinction for the two traditions. The Harp and Crown can be found on the murals of Belfast and on the cap badge of the Royal Irish Regiment, while the Harp symbolising Ireland can be found in Republican iconography and is used to symbolise the state in the Republic of Ireland. The RUC also inherited the rank insignia of the former force which had developed a rank structure, separate and distinct from those of the GB forces.

The new Northern government in the mid-1920s held the Harp and Crown of the former RIC to be too Irish to be adopted by the RUC and attempted to substitute a new crest comprising using the new arms of Northern Ireland, a central red hand of Ulster against the background of the red cross of the flag of St George (*see illustration on page 28*). The RUC Inspector General and many of the new force were ex-RIC members who were proud of their links and continuity with the former force and rejected the new crest and badge. In the face of sustained opposition to the new design the government felt compelled to back down and abandon the project. The design of the Red Hand and Cross, like that of the Harp, has been used by both traditions in the north of Ireland, the only variable being the inclusion or not of the British Crown.

Reform of the RUC as a result of the recommendations of the Hunt Committee in 1969 led to the introduction of the GB police ranks, but retained the Harp and Crown badge and insignia. The onset of the 'Troubles' and the police casualties sustained as a result led the Harp and Crown of the RUC to take on a new significance, not as a symbol of loyalty but as one of sacrifice. As the Harp and Crown was also worn by the Ulster Defence Regiment, an army regiment which assisted the police with local security and which sustained many casualties in the 'Troubles', the device took on a wider importance for many in the Unionist community. During the debate over the future shape of policing in the late 1990s a lengthy campaign was launched to in an attempt save the name of the force and its badge. In the end it was recommended that

The badge of the RIC, as adopted by the RUC in 1922

The proposed new crest for the RUC, 1923

force adopt a badge and insignia devoid of any British or Irish symbolism.

Speculation over the form of the new badge was ended when the new Northern Ireland Policing Board decided on a compromise design to include symbols drawn from both communities and adopted a badge in the shape of a sunburst with a central red Cross of St Patrick. This was surrounded by six quarters, each for a county of Northern Ireland, in which were illustrated a British crown, an Irish harp and shamrock, the scales of justice, an olive branch for peace and a torch for truth (*see page 30*). Rank insignia also changed with the loss of the crown worn by senior ranks and its substitution by the Cross of St Patrick. The crossed tipstaves worn by the rank of Assistant Chief Constable and above similarly lost their crowns to produce an apolitical design.

History and records

It has been said that the Irish are good at destroying their own history and indeed many invaluable archives were lost in the partition of Ireland in 1922 and ensuing Civil War in the south. The disbandment of the Royal Irish Constabulary in 1922 led to the fragmentation and destruction of its records.[1] While the Public Records Office for Northern Ireland was established in 1923, security concerns meant that many historical police records were retained by their originating departments and not transferred. The onset of the 'Troubles' in 1969 exacerbated the situation with regard to security and led to a reluctance on the part of the police to release records and a corresponding reluctance by the PRO in Belfast to open records for research, even when copies were freely available for inspection at Kew. At the time of writing PSNI still has no standardised protocol for the transfer of historical records to the Public Records Office.

The 60th anniversary of the RUC in 1982 was the catalyst for the setting up of a historical society and museum. More importantly, the museum was established as an operational part of the RUC with an ex-Superintendent appointed to a permanent post of Curator. As the museum was an integrated part of the force, the Curator was allowed unimpeded access to police complexes and stations, enabling him to save many archives from destruction. These included crime registers, station inspection books, officers' journals, patrol books and station diaries and notebooks, the earliest dating from the 1830s. Unlike many

PSNI crest, from 2001

GB forces, which have undergone repeated amalgamations, with the destruction of personnel records, the advantage of a single centralised force has been that the personnel records of the RUC have been preserved intact running from 1922 and have now been transferred to the museum. The 'personalia' of former members of the RUC members have also been donated to the museum.

The momentous changes in policing in the Province, with the removal of the RUC name and symbols, led to a sense of grievance and loss, experienced by not only police officers and their families but also in the wider Unionist community. In recognition of this and to preserve the name and achievements of the RUC, the Police Act of 2000 established the RUC George Cross Foundation which has opened a police memorial garden at the PSNI headquarters site and will be responsible for a planned new purpose-built museum. Police heritage in Northern Ireland is therefore well served by having an established museum in place and a new champion in the RUC GC Foundation.

As a police service, the PSNI is probably the most closely observed and scrutinised in the world and is entering a new era of transparency and accountability which will benefit its archival heritage. The onset of the Freedom of Information Act has prompted an information audit of the entire organisation to establish an Information Asset Register. The entire operation will be benchmarked by having outside oversight to guard against the danger that some branches may withhold records, or intentionally destroy them to prevent them becoming public. An integrated records management strategy along with the appointment of a dedicated Records Manager will ensure the historical records are identified at an early stage for permanent preservation. On the negative side however, the paramountcy of security along with the need to protect the lives of individuals has undoubtedly led to many archives being destroyed. Other factors would be the results of terrorist bombings of stations, space requirements, ignorance and disinterest. The sense of hurt over the loss of the RUC name and its symbols and the desire to preserve the reputation of the former force and the memory of fellow police officers who lost their lives to terrorism may also have played a part.

The history of policing the north of Ireland may be troubled, but it is one which is unique and well worth preserving.

Note
1. For an account of the fate of some RIC records: 'The Missing Personnel Records of the RIC' by Gerard O'Brien in *Irish Historical Studies* vol. xxxi, no.124, Nov. 1999.

Chapter Two

The Metropolitan and City Police Orphanage and the Collective Memory of the Police Community in London

Stefania Bernini

The last fifteen years have seen an increasing interest in the 'social history' of the English police and the daily reality of policing, particularly in the twentieth century. This growing body of research has showed the relevance of looking at police organisations in relation, not only to the history of criminology and the social justice system, but also the history of labour and social relations in modern Britain.[1] The experience which is presented here is an example of research which, although based on primary evidence produced almost entirely by a police organisation, aims to make a contribution to debates taking place outside as well as inside police studies. Its main resource is a unique and valuable archive.

The research project on the history of the London Metropolitan and City Police Orphanage, which operated in Twickenham between 1870 and 1937, started in the autumn of 2002 as the result of the collaboration established between the European Centre for the Study of Policing at the Open University and the Metropolitan and City Police Orphans Fund. In these two years, the research has provided insights into a number of areas, including the family lives of London policemen, approaches to workers' welfare and paternalist interventions within the police, gender relations in the home and in the workplace from the late nineteenth century, approaches to childcare and education, and the relationship between professionalism and definitions of respectable masculinity. The research, now in its final stage, suggests that the London Orphanage can be studied as a major example of paternalism in the London area, which was able to provide support to policemen's families in the event of the loss of their main income but also established a degree of control over policemen and their families and promoted a respectable image for the police in the capital.

The main source of evidence for the research is provided by the records of the orphanage, now held by the Metropolitan and City Police Orphans Fund. Throughout the research these have been integrated into the information provided by the records held in the museums of the Metropolitan Police and of the City of London Police, and by an extensive use of contemporary newspapers and magazines. A further level of analysis has been provided by interviews conducted with some of the people who entered the orphanage during its final years of activity, some of whom could be traced thanks to their remaining links with the Metropolitan and City Police Orphans Fund and with the museum of the London Metropolitan Police.

As well as confirming the relevance of police records to research outside the history of policing and the importance of preserving and making them more easily accessible to the larger research community, the work carried out during the last two years has shown how working on documents from the past remains essential if we are to preserve and foster a sense of communal belonging and collective memories. These have proved extraordinarily resilient amongst those who went through the police orphanage, who still speak of the strong ties forged as young people and of the sense of belonging to one of London's largest working communities which was transmitted through the orphanage.

The project itself was only possible thanks to the constant support provided by the Metropolitan and City Police Orphans Fund, which has preserved and kept alive the archive of the orphanage since its closure in 1937 (in particular

METROPOLITAN AND CITY POLICE ORPHANAGE

TWICKENHAM

Patron

His Most Gracious Majesty King Edward VII

CERTIFICATE ON LEAVING THE ORPHANAGE

I Hereby Certify that Robert Davey was Maintained and Educated in this Orphanage from Sep 16, 04 to Xmas 1907. On leaving he was in CLASS I STANDARD VI His CONDUCT was Very good INDUSTRY Very good and his PROGRESS Very satisfactory.

SIGNED A.M. Edwards Chairman.

DATE Decr 13th, 1907.

Copy of certificate received on leaving the orphanage, 1907

assisting in a number of genealogical enquiries), as well as by the present curators of the museums of the Metropolitan Police and the City of London Police. There is little doubt, however, that the research would have been much poorer without the invaluable contribution of those who were willing to share their recollections of the years spent in the orphanage.

The orphanage and its 'orphans'

The Police Orphanage opened in October 1870 in Twickenham, with the aim 'to afford relief to as many of the destitute orphans of members of the Metropolitan Police Force as the funds will allow of; to provide them with clothing, maintenance, and education; and to place them out in situations where the prospect of an honest livelihood shall be secured'.[2] The benefits were extended to the orphans of the City of London police in the following year.

The name of the institution reflected an understanding of the term 'orphan' which was common in Victorian and Edwardian culture, as someone who was deprived of only one parent, in this case normally the father. The great majority of the children admitted to the orphanage still had mothers who were not only alive but who tried to maintain regular contacts with them; in a minority of cases fathers also survived, and admission to the orphanage was granted on the basis of their inability to work due to medical reasons. More generally, the term 'orphan' made reference to a state of vulnerability and disadvantage for which the police community assumed responsibility.[3]

The growing uneasiness felt towards such a definition, however, became obvious from the 1920s, when the orphanage started to be increasingly referred to as 'Fortescue school', both in letters of reference written for the boys leaving the institution during its last years and in everyday discourse. This was confirmed by a number of interviewees, according to whom mothers never spoke of 'the orphanage', referring instead to 'the school'. What can be read as mothers' desire to re-affirm their role in the life of their children against stigmatising definitions also showed the determination of the police authorities to distinguish their institution from other charitable interventions addressed to deprived children, first of all on the grounds that the orphanage aimed to provide 'a type of boarding school training and education which is superior to that obtainable at ordinary elementary schools'.[4]

From the 1920s, however, the merits of institutional assistance started to be questioned and what had been presented fifty years earlier as advantages not obtainable through a system of allowances paid to mothers were considered in a more critical light.[5] As the orphanage confronted changing perceptions of child care, shifting pedagogical approaches, and an increasing interest in the psychological development of children, its healthy surroundings and sport and educational facilities started to be measured against the potential damage provoked by the separation of young children from their mothers, as well as against the spiralling costs of bringing the home up to modern standards.[6]

Having experienced years of overcrowding until the First World War, by the early 1930s 'much persuasion' was needed 'to induce mothers to send their children to the Orphanage'. In order 'to keep up the numbers', children had been admitted 'under the original minimum age and kept on over the original compulsory leaving age'; contrary to rules, 'the children of mothers who had remarried' had been retained together with 'some children whose fathers are still alive, but medically unfit for work'.[7] After years of struggling with numbers, the decision to close the orphanage in 1937 reflected growing economic difficulties as well as changes in perceptions concerning child welfare education and family relationships and the changes which had taken place in the position of policemen and their families.

Throughout its history, the orphanage exhibited aspects typical of paternalist intervention aimed to defuse tensions within a workforce which was still badly paid and enjoying limited welfare benefits. Yet this was combined with the promotion of workers solidarity among London's police, by means of their direct participation to the financing of the institution through weekly contributions and the frequent appeal to their support in a number of initiatives launched by the organisation. Fundraising proved often a highly popular enterprise, able to mobilise entire divisions, and initiatives included sport and musical events, particularly memorable among which remain the concerts organised by the Police Minstrels from the first years of the orphanage and until its closure. The popular donation boxes placed in every police station helped to promote the popularity of the orphanage among the general public. In a number of cases, donations from members of the public came accompanied by notes expressing gratitude for the help received from the police. The Royal Patronage granted in 1871 to the orphanage confirmed the idea that this should occupy 'a very high position amongst the charitable institutions of the country'. The stream of distinguished visitors (and donors) to the orphanage, which included the higher echelons of the London Police as well as royalty and political personalities, testified to the success of a strategy aimed not only to provide welfare to policemen's families but also to increase the prestige and standing of the London police.

The orphanage and the collective memory of the police community in London

By the time the orphanage closed in 1937, more than 2,000 children had passed through the institution; they received different kinds of academic education, moral teaching, physical and professional training according to their age and gender, as well as to the period in which they entered the home. The records they left help to map not only individual biographies, but also the changes taking place in the social circumstances of their families throughout the years and in the definition of what represented a 'desirable' path to adulthood for young working-class people.

Moreover, the documents make a valuable contribution to the study of orphanages as institutions, their place in child care and the different sets of values and expectations attached to them. This is a particularly valuable contribution, since while studies looking critically at changing approaches to childhood and social policies for children have seen a significant expansion in the last thirty years, few works have looked specifically and critically at orphanages as a specific kind of institution and their interaction with changing notions of social and political responsibility towards young people and in relation to paternalist interventions towards workers' families.

The importance of the Metropolitan and City Police Orphanage's archive is greatly enhanced in this respect by the fact that its collections have been preserved nearly untouched throughout the years, mainly thanks to the continuity existing between the orphanage and the Orphans' Fund which was opened after its closure and in whose hands the minute books of the Board of Managers, the annual reports and the registers of applications and admission (which constitute the core of the collections) have since remained. Furthermore, the written

Cover of an information booklet for widows of officers of the Metropolitan and City police forces, published in 1935

Metropolitan Police
Athletic Association

Annual Concert

at the

Central Hall, Westminster

IN AID OF THE METROPOLITAN
AND CITY POLICE ORPHANS FUND

on

Friday, 5th November, 1948

at 7 p.m.

President:
Sir HAROLD SCOTT, K.C.B., K.B.E. (Commissioner)
Chairman M.P.A.A.:
Major P. R. MARGETSON, C.V.O., M.C. (Assistant Commissioner)
CHORAL SOCIETY:
Chairman: Supt. F. H. ARCHER. *Hon. Secretary:* S.D. Insp. T. O'DONNELL
METROPOLITAN POLICE CENTRAL BAND:
Chairman: R. HOWE, Esq., M.C. (Assistant Commissioner)
Director of Music: Mr. R. BARSOTTI, A.R.C.M. (late Queen's Royal Regt.)
Hon. Secretary: Supt. R. S. LOBB
Hon. Secretary M.P.A.A.: Insp. G. MALKIN

Leaflet advertising the Annual Concert organised by the Metropolitan Police in 1948; fund-raising initiatives in support of the Metropolitan and City Orphans Fund continued after the closure of the Orphanage in 1935

records left by the orphanage can still be tested and questioned through the memories of those who experienced life there. An 'old scholar association', which existed until the mid 1980s, provided for many years occasions to meet for those who were once together in the orphanage and has been vital in preserving the memory of this institution and in transmitting a powerful sense of shared experience.

Now that the organisation no longer exists and fewer of the orphans are still alive, the importance of working on the history of the orphanage, through its written records as well as through the memories of those who were part of that history, is further enhanced.

The eagerness of those whom I have interviewed to tell their stories, not only of the years spent inside the orphanage but of their experiences as the children of London's policemen and often, especially in the case of men, as policemen themselves in later years, compel us to preserve, and wherever possible to collect the memories of this still relatively recent past, preserving the records left by one of London's larger working communities and making them available to private and academic researchers and students. The documents held by the Metropolitan and City Police Orphans Fund, by the Metropolitan Police Museum, and by the Museum of the City Police provide a wealth of information which is essential to the understanding not only of the history of policing but to the social history of London as well.

Notes

1. Among the examples of this historiography are C. Emsley, *The English Police, A Political and Social History*, (London: Longman, 1991); Barbara Weinberger, *Keeping the Peace? Policing Strikes in Britain, 1906–1926*, (Oxford: Berg, 1991) and idem, *The Best Police in the World: an Oral History of English Policing from the 1930s to the 1960s*, (Aldershot: Scolar Press, 1995); Mike Brogden, *On the Mersey Beat: Policing Liverpool between the Wars*, Oxford: OUP, 1991 and specifically for the London police, Haia Shpayer Makov, *The Making of a Policeman, a social history of a labour force in metropolitan London, 1829–1914*, (Aldershot: Ashgate, 2002).
2. *Rules for the Government and Management of the Metropolitan Police Orphanage*, 1870, para.2, p.2.
3. L.Peters, *Orphan Texts, Victorian Orphans, Culture and Empire*, (Manchester: Manchester University Press, 2000), p.1.
4. *Committee of Enquiry as to the Necessity for the Retention of the Metropolitan and City Police Orphanage*, Report, 1 June, 1934, para.12e, p.13.
5. Ibid., para. 13a–13k, pp.14–16.
6. On the growing 'psychologising' of the child, see H. Hendrick, *Child Welfare, England 1872–1989*, (London: Routledge, 1994), pp.149–150.
7. *Committee of Enquiry as to the Necessity for the Retention of the Metropolitan and City Police Orphanage*, para.13e, p.13.

Chapter Three

The Police Vehicle Enthusiasts' Club: Working to Record Police Transport History

Paddy Carpenter

Just as the history of the UK police service is inextricably bound up with the social history of the last two centuries, it also interfaces crucially with studies of other subject areas, few more visibly interdependent than that of transport, particularly road transport. Indeed the whole image of policing has been defined by modes of transport, from bobbies on bicycles, through mounted police in public order situations, to the electronically sophisticated 'eye in the sky' aircraft. From the time that motor patrols began in 1930 and especially since Unit Beat policing and panda cars put more and more officers in cars from 1965, the story of the police has gone hand in hand with that of first the British and eventually the international motor industry, and the development of each has impacted the other. Yet British police transport is a subject very poorly recorded and equally little studied, with very little published until the late nineties.[1]

Where have all the records gone?
It used to be traditional that new vehicles were photographed on entering service, frequently in a long line-up with their crews at attention. Likewise motorised units, assembled during annual parades for Her Majesty's Inspectors of Constabulary, were recorded on film and technological advances or new policing incentives also occasioned photography. Thankfully, many such images have survived, although equally we know that in amalgamations much evidence was destroyed, through lack of interest or foresight, and in some cases as an act of vindictiveness as one force 'eliminated' another that had been regarded as a rival or a thorn in its side. There was also no doubt a degree of unauthorised 'liberation' as described at the June 2004 conference by Clive Emsley. Written records, not surprisingly, fared rather worse and very little seems to have survived (even in those forces that have enjoyed a continuity of existence) about vehicle acquisitions and disposals. In most cases fleet sizes,

Dorset Motor Patrols, c.1935

types, dates, modifications, allocations, utilisation patterns and financial aspects, (to name but some), are all lost forever; indeed our impression is that in many forces there seems to be a continuing policy of erasing such details after a very brief interval.

Pieces of the jigsaw may be found in published sources; and the archives of newspapers and periodicals represent a mountain of material from which suitably dedicated researchers may hope eventually to sift some nuggets. There is small doubt, however, that gaping holes in our knowledge remain, and although the picture varies with geography, in general the 70s and 80s are perhaps the worst covered. Some of the best and most crucial unofficial records are those made by police officers themselves. Fortunately there are many who have made a habit of photographing themselves and their colleagues with the vehicles they drove. Sometimes of only 'snapshot' quality, and with the crew member often infuriatingly obliterating some interesting detail, these pictures and the officers' recollections may yet often be the sole evidence of an important purchase or allocation. Mention of the officers' memories sounds the warning note. Much of the unrecorded information exists only in the heads of those lived the story. If not written down, it is lost when they pass on, and how many of their albums of 'boring' police car pictures go in the dustbin accompanied by the infamous words 'No-one's interested in those old things.'

A positive step
1987 saw an unlikely move taken in the right direction when a small club was formed for those engaged in making accurate scale models of police vehicles. Accuracy demands evidence and so the collection of pictures and details was a natural progression for some involved. Archiving became established as an activity in its own right and the club quickly adopted its present name – Police Vehicle Enthusiasts' Club, more usually known as PVEC and pronounced Pee-Vec. A crucial development was that members started to record and photograph contemporary vehicles; important in that many forces were no longer troubling to do so. In the world of police transport, vehicles are replaced with extraordinary frequency and with individual liveries and equipment changing at an increasing rate, the notion that 'History Begins This Afternoon' is nowhere truer.

As a Club based in the UK, the information we have accumulated is inevitably and appropriately UK-biased, but we now have international membership and information exchange. It is fair to say that every single person on our membership list of about 280 people worldwide will have some form of archive. It may be a few packets of photographs in a drawer, in many cases it will be a series of annotated picture albums and in several instances it will be a huge collection of images in a variety of forms, comprehensively indexed with supporting information on a powerful computer database. As in any organisation, people have their specialist fields of study and so we have experts in most aspects whether geographic, time-specific, type, make or model oriented. We have members who cover police aircraft, watercraft, horses and horse-drawn units; I have yet to find a specialist on police pedal cycles, but I have no doubt that there is one some-

Owners use picture archives to ensure accuracy of restorations. Left, a genuine Somerset & Bath Constabulary Jaguar 340; right, a replica Bristol Constabulary Wolseley 6/110 Mk II

where and when that person finds out about us and joins, I personally have 127 images for him or her to identify.

The study of vehicles leads inevitably to a consideration of the equipment developed for them, of which the most significant category would undoubtedly be that of communications. John Bunker's excellent book *From Rattle to Radio* shows the vital role that the development of radio played and continues to play in influencing mobile police operations; a process which continues with radar, GPS, CAD, ANPR and an avalanche of other acronyms, while relatively low-tech inventions such as VASCAR have played and do play their part in the story.[2] Our subject also overlaps with other specialist groups. For example, uniform and personal equipment is contiguous with transport history but researched in enormous detail by the Police Insignia Collectors' Association (PICA). Equally, much important motorcycle knowledge is held within the Historic Police Motorcycle Group.

The third and most recent strand to PVEC's activities has been our almost incidental recruiting of people who found themselves restoring former police vehicles, or in some cases making accurate replicas. The whole business of finding and preserving such vehicles has itself been almost entirely accidental, very much an example of what Alice Stewart memorably described as 'fate-dictated survival' (see Chapter 13 below). Hardly any vehicles have been preserved because of any conscious policy or intent to identify a specific subject important enough to save. Usually preservation has occurred because having bought a classic car or even a car for daily use, the new owner has happened to discover odd filled holes in the roof, or extra fuses and disconnected wiring; or any of a number of clues that hint at a former career. In what must be a relatively small number of cases, the owner has reacted in what might be deemed a fairly eccentric way, because in choosing to restore a car to an in-service condition, a step is taken which drastically reduces the use which can be made of a vehicle. A fully marked and police car with lights does not get taken out for a casual run on any sunny Sunday, even with the lights and insignia legally covered. It is therefore little short of miraculous that such a wealth of thoroughly representative and important machinery has managed to survive for our enjoyment and the education of generations to come.

What PVEC is doing
For many years a travelling 'PVEC Road Show' exhibition of police models and pictures has successfully attended a great variety of police and other events, either in conjunction with preserved cars or independently. From seeing our members display their restored cars at Car Shows, Emergency Service Events and Police Service Open Days, we are aware that preserved vehicles generate extraordinary goodwill for the police service. They are a valuable PR tool in that when presented, they seem to engender an automatic respect for law and order, even in the unlikeliest of observers and are particularly appealing to the young. They undoubtedly encourage good citizenship, they have certainly assisted with recruiting in many cases and they most definitely contribute to an appreciation of heritage and history, the more so by being live, working exhibits. The engines run, the sirens wail and the lights flash, in a way that

A Ford Zephyr 6 Mk IV 4WD experimental demonstrator, a Rover ex-Met Special Escort Group, a Kent Granada Mk II Srs II and a Hampshire Rover P6 3500, once the official car of Lord Mountbatten on the Isle of Wight. PVEC members own police cars from seven decades starting with the 1930s

museum items cannot do; especially those tucked away in a dusty, ill-lit, cramped corner of a reserve collection visitable only on several months' advance application, which was the reported fate of a car at one time promised to the Club.

PVEC's main challenge is to fill in the gaps in coverage and try to encourage the preservation of significant makes or models as yet unrepresented in the heritage fleet, where they are still to be found. Another pressing task, with the sad demise of many of the distinctive liveries which have brightened the 1980s and 90s, is to keep those alive on appropriate units. Both such objectives require targeted preservation and we, as a body, have acted on both counts, albeit where fate has given us the opportunity to do so. In 2002 we were offered custody of a retiring Merseyside traffic car as a Club flagship to publicise our preservation incentives. The practical advantages of having a car transferred in an 'as in ser-

Another one saved! Probably the last surviving genuine Hillman Imp panda car. The Club itself bought this car in half an hour from the Internet, in order to ensure that it will be restored as befits its unique history

vice' condition, without stripping and re-equipping were obvious and the PR significance for both us and the Merseyside Police was extraordinary. After months of planning to attract sponsorship, and with the move endorsed at the highest levels within the force, it was mysteriously withdrawn, without any credible explanation, days before coming to fruition. We have never been told why, but it is clear that there must have been some intervention from an unsympathetic or ill-informed source.

Collectively indignant and now very cautious about sharing our plans, we were shown the way forward in 2003 by an individual member who used his own contacts and dogged persistence to persuade Avon and Somerset to donate their last surviving Vauxhall Senator, which otherwise faced being destroyed. Unfolding events then gave us an opportunity to approach Gloucestershire Constabulary, with the result that a Volvo 850 T-5, one of the County's first Armed Response Vehicles, now belongs to PVEC for restoration back to its original and now extinct paint scheme. In a flurry of recent activity, the Club has bought, in order to save as a police vehicle, what is likely to be the last surviving Hillman Imp panda car, formerly of the Kent Constabulary. Meanwhile individuals have targeted vehicles to preserve; one being a Derbyshire Ford Transit Police Support Unit (PSU) carrier. The force co-operated magnificently with the new owner and the result is that the first PSU in active preservation is now at events, complete with windscreen grille, internal cage and full force markings.

The small minority who in ignorance dismiss preservationists as would-be policemen or look for security dangers in the existence of heritage vehicles have not studied the facts. Many of the owners are themselves serving or retired officers, who certainly would have nothing to do with anything or anyone less than totally serious, responsible and secure. At the last count 60 members own 107 preserved cars, motorcycles and vans, a truly 'living museum' of the police service, which costs the service nothing to create and maintain, other than the donation of odd items of normally obsolete equipment which otherwise would be destined for scrap.

The Club has given great thought to the subject of photographs, and prepared a major report comparing the present situation, where a large number of private collections co-exist, complementing and overlapping each other, with the perhaps ideal situation, where a central accessible collection would contain everything that is known to exist. Whilst technical advances constantly make the latter more possible, formidable practical obstacles make it unachievable in the immediate future. Aside from considerations of copyright, the task of persuading owners to participate, and then cataloguing, copying and making copies readily available to participants is one that would require the full-time commitment of at least one person and possibly more. Under the Club's present circumstances, this cannot be funded, but there are ways that this could change, one of which will be alluded to later.

In order to dip a toe into the unknown waters of co-operation, an incentive called Interpool has been introduced, under which a member prepares a document containing all the information he or she has discovered on a chosen subject. This is sent to all those interested in contributing, who then compare the document with their own archive. On the basis of their findings, they supply

A line-up of ex-Sussex vehicles at the Hampshire Constabulary Families' Day. Already in 2004, PVEC has supplied displays for Hampshire, Gloucestershire, Gwent, South Wales, the Met, Avon & Somerset, Dorset and Merseyside forces, as well as for numerous car shows, 999 and other events

corrections and additions which are returned to the originator. He or she collates all the changes and incorporates them into a revised document, which is then re-circulated to all participants, while a summary will appear in our quarterly magazine *Sidestripe*. In theory the sum total of members' knowledge on that topic is now shared by all those with an interest in it. This the best chance we've got to pool our knowledge, and the response to the first chosen area (the early generations of panda vehicles, characterised in most places by a blue and white colour scheme) has been extremely encouraging and has unearthed some very interesting examples which might not have come to light without the spotlight being turned onto the subject. This success will be repeated by other members with further suitably-chosen topics.

As a consequence of the Club's moving to cater more appropriately for the preserved vehicle sector, it became imperative to look at our existing Preserved Vehicle Register, which comprised two spring binders containing responses to a questionnaire and a three-page list distilled from them. These records have now been computerised and augmented with many additional items, the ostensible aim being to incorporate all the preserved or potentially preserved former police vehicles in the country, whether owned by members or not. When it is realised that hundreds of vehicles are decommissioned each month it will be clear that the aim is impossible to achieve, but such an approach should capture virtually every vehicle that is fully restored or undergoing work, and at least some of those that could be restored and are in the hands of owners who recognise their significance. This document is of course of enormous help in organising the preservation side of the Club, and is of great importance to anyone who wishes to know of the existence of vehicles, not least police forces themselves, who are constantly holding events at which heritage vehicles are a desirable bonus.

I feel some satisfaction and no little irony that the Merseyside Police are among the many forces who have enjoyed, at their request, the presence of a number of PVEC vehicles at their Force Open Days. The current status of the Register shows 359 preserved cars and vans, 99 motorcycles and 197 known owners (bearing in mind that some enthusiasts own several vehicles). Most of these vehicles are fully and authentically equipped inside and out, thus presenting a real insight into the policing conditions of the era. For example, it was for many years a practice in some forces to specify cars without heaters, or even remove or disable them, often with the excuse of saving weight, but with the real and sometimes plainly-stated intention of not making conditions too comfortable and 'soft' for the rank and file.

The way forward
At least two Club Officers are considering the idea of a Police Transport Museum as a project for their retirement, and Charles Griffiths and other speakers at the June 2004 conference provided very valuable information and advice on some of the complexities to be encountered. This project has already had one set-back: an offer, local authority-inspired, to take over a historic, listed redundant police station, in a thriving tourist town, was looking quite promising until local political empire-building reared its head.

The growing numbers of preserved police vehicles being seen on the event

Cars built between 1953 and 1989 greeted HRH Prince Michael of Kent when he opened the Tri-Service Workshops at Gloucester in March 2004. Most had either served in the West or were types that had been used by Gloucestershire Constabulary

circuit are certainly helping to ensure that, after years of neglect, the subject is emerging from its position as the Cinderella of transport history. With high profile contributions such as those made by PVEC to the Queen's Golden Jubilee Parade and to a recent Royal Visit and by the Met Traffic Museum's cars for the Met's own 175th Birthday Parade, those in top jobs are now appreciating the value of heritage vehicles and the two-way benefits of co-operating with the preservation movement. More donations and joint preservation/restoration ventures will doubtless follow. Contacts are also being established with workshops to try and save obsolete equipment like blue lights and radio selectors, which are vital for restoration projects, but which are routinely thrown into skips as being of no further value. As was said at the conference with regard to paper records, 'Give us the opportunity to save everything. We are uniquely placed to know whether some item is worthy of keeping for a future project or not.' We can collect. We can store. And our Club Equipment Officer is ready for telephone calls.

The presentation and the discussion on the Freedom of Information Act offered the spectre of the police service potentially under enormous strain in attempting to respond to FIA requests. Unless we misunderstood what was said, it sounds as if anyone could submit a request, for example, for all information and material held relating to former vehicles. Obviously currently-owned assets would be made the subject of an exemption on security grounds, but vehicles sold or scrapped would, if the Act means anything, be open to disclosure. To avoid at least the time-consuming chore of responding for evermore to requests from enthusiasts seeking the same information, it would make sound sense, it would seem, for forces without separate arms-length museums or historical societies to donate their transport records over an agreed age to PVEC and to refer all such enquiries to the Club for attention. The Club would undertake to respond to requests in an appropriate way, but would not be bound by the provisions of the Act. As forces that had followed this procedure would no longer possess their historic transport archive, they too would be free of the Act in this respect and could not be forced to reproduce material for every applicant. By agreement they could of course access their former records whenever required. PVEC would be in a position to charge a reasonable fee for information supplied to enquirers and such fees would enable the costs of running a central archive to be met. In short, all parties gain advantages, but without legal constraints and the prospect of penalties. I would propose that ACPO considers this strategy in good time for it to be recommended for implementation. It would seem perhaps to make sense for societies like the Police History Society and PICA similarly to consider the possibility of offering to steward such sections of records as might be deemed appropriate to their areas of study.

PVEC's delegates left the conference with some confidence that interest from such a wide spectrum of organisations indicated that the subject of police heritage was at last receiving the consideration due to it. Our organisation and activities go from strength to strength, but one never knows what pitfalls exist round the next corner. Publicity given to a lone individual, quite unconnected with our Club and with interests far removed from historical preservation, who has re-equipped a former police car and, apparently by his own admission used it inappropriately, could conceivably undo years of patient effort by genuine enthusiasts, thanks to irresponsible press reporting. It was also with sinking hearts that we heard that the sad story of the Met Museum and its archives appears to be back at square one, with the building at Charlton, as we understand it, closed abruptly and the contracts of the custodians not renewed. The ominous clouds which rolled around Clive Emsley's opening remarks have not disappeared nearly as much as we had hoped.

Notes
1. One rare exception was published by conference attendee, Roy D. Ingleton, *Police vehicles of the world* (London: Ian Allen, 1980).
2. John Bunker, *From Rattle to Radio* (Studley: K.A.F.Brewin, 1988).

Part Two

Problems and Pitfalls

IMPORTANT
This is a confidential publication for use of Police only and must not be copied or published without authority.

NEW SCOTLAND YARD,
LONDON,
S.W.1

STATE FUNERAL OF THE RIGHT HONOURABLE SIR WINSTON LEONARD SPENCER CHURCHILL, K.G., O.M., C.H.

1. **Introduction.** This pamphlet is issued to all ranks on duty in connection with the State Funeral. Its purpose is to outline the more important duties and responsibilities of police and to provide a ready reference to the sequence of events and situation of various services. Absorb this information and do your utmost to enhance the reputation of the British Police for helpfulness and courtesy.

2. **Duties of Police.** In addition to their normal duties, police employed on or near the line of route will be responsible for :—
   (i) keeping the Processional routes clear and protecting the persons using them,
   (ii) ensuring the safety of spectators in public places, and
   (iii) giving help where necessary to members of the public.

3. **Formation and Keeping of Police Line.** The route of the Procession will be kept by police standing in line below the kerb unless otherwise directed.

   The route (except on the South Bank) is being lined throughout by the Fighting Services about one pace from the kerb unless otherwise shown in the Operation Order.

   The public will not be allowed to pass between troops lining the route and police, and in no circumstances will spectators be allowed to stand in front of the police line.

   Members of the St. John Ambulance Brigade are to be given facilities to carry out their duties. When not so employed they may stand in line with police, *but not at closer intervals* than 10 yards. Surplus First Aid personnel must remain off the Processional route.

   Members of the public wishing to take photographs or cine films are not to be allowed in front of the police line.

   It is important that police frequently watch the crowd behind their line, in order to detect anything of a suspicious nature.

   The police line must be held and spectators asked to stand firm until the troops lining the route have marched away.

   As far as possible, the principle to be adopted is that the available space along the route must be filled from the rear, use being made of the side streets. Lateral movement will, whenever circumstances permit, be along parallel streets and not along the route itself.

   After the procession has passed it is anticipated that large numbers of members of the public will disperse to Victoria Embankment or the South Bank area to view the later processions at Waterloo and on the River Thames. Certain police personnel may be required to assist in controlling the movement of such crowds, and it is essential that police maintain their positions until otherwise directed.

4. **Saluting.** Officers below the rank of Inspector will not salute but will stand to attention when Her Majesty The Queen, other Members of the Royal Family and the funeral cortege are passing and when they are passing or are being passed by uncased Standards or Colours. Inspectors and above will salute.

5. **Procession.**
   The Processional route will be :—
   (a) New Palace Yard
   Parliament Square (east side)
   Parliament Street
   Whitehall
   Charing Cross (east side of King Charles Statue Island)
   Strand (south side)
   Fleet Street
   Ludgate Circus
   Ludgate Hill
   St. Paul's Cathedral
   St. Paul's Churchyard
   Cannon Street
   Eastcheap
   Great Tower Street
   Byward Street
   Tower Hill and
   Tower Pier.

   (b) The funeral cortege will then proceed by the River Thames from Tower Pier to Festival Hall Pier.
   (c) From Festival Hall Pier the route will be :—
   Across the Riverside Walk and ramp to Festival Hall site
   Festival Hall Service Road
   Belvedere Road.
   Concert Hall Approach
   York Road
   Exit Road from Waterloo Station

6. **Military Arrangements.** Members of the Fighting Services lining the route will be in position at various times between 8.35 a.m. and 11.15 a.m. Guards of Honour are being mounted at New Palace Yard, Tower Wharf and Tower Hill, and Military Bands will be taking part in the procession.

Orders for the funeral of Winston Churchill, 1965. Police records can give a useful slant on current affairs as well as social history

Chapter Four

British Police Forces' Archiving Policies in 2003

Chris A. Williams and Clive Emsley

Before 1999, the London Metropolitan Police reported directly to the Home Office and were thus covered by the Public Records Acts. British police outside London did not, and are not covered. Thus the documentary evidence they have left is poor. This has been one factor leading to a distorted historiography of the British police which has focused too closely on developments in the capital.[1] Without adequate records from the provinces, this distortion is likely to endure. Provincial forces have played a key role in many headline political events such as the General Strike and the 1974 and 1984/85 miners' strikes. Their records are also a way in to the social history of all manner of issues.[2] This chapter will look at the way that the vast majority of British police forces currently organise their ongoing production of historical records.

There are 50 or so provincial police forces. Most are the product of a process of amalgamation from smaller forces: at their peak in the 1880s there were over 200: the most significant contractions happened between 30 and 40 years ago. This loss of institutional continuity has led to the loss of the records of many smaller forces. It has also created forces that have more than one local record office in their area: for example, the West Mercia force covers Herefordshire, Worcestershire and Shropshire. Provincial police are not national, but nor are they legally part of local government, and thus not subject to the archive provisions of the 1972 Local Government Act.[3] This is a consequence of their constitutional development in the twentieth century, which saw them, with the support of the Home Office, effectively break free from accountability as part of local government, without central government acknowledging that they were in large part now under its control.[4]

The police have a vested interest in secrecy for several reasons, some highly justifiable. Legally, they need to avoid contempt of court for *sub judice* proceedings, and to keep within the provisions of the 1996 Criminal Procedure and Investigations Act.[5] Operationally, there is an imperative to maintain security, which can sometimes literally be a life and death issue, for example in the case of payments to informers. Above and beyond this, police have a strong symbolic attachment to control of information about the way that they work, especially information about the way that the job is done in practice rather than in theory. Malcolm Young, an anthropologist who was also a Detective Superintendent, wrote that for a police force, academic study can be a threat:

> The fear is always that the outside will be presented with the chance to gain knowledge and power at the expense of the institution; although this is often only obliquely implied.[6]

It is worth noting that Young was referring mainly to his experience in the police service in the 1970s and 1980s. Like many other organisations, many police forces are keen to talk about a new spirit of openness to scrutiny.[7] Some individuals within these forces may well sincerely believe this, but it does not alter the fact that few organisations welcome outside critical scrutiny, and fewer are more dependent on a culture of insider knowledge than are the police.[8] Furthermore, the British police derive much of their legitimacy from an appeal to their history, featuring the democratic heritage of the office of citizen-constable, combined with the contradictory legacy of Peel's disciplined but unarmed force.[9]

This report derives from the follow-up to a survey of provincial police archives by Ian Bridgeman and Clive Emsley in 1989. This led to the publication of a catalogue of the archives of the Police Forces of England and Wales. In it, the authors concluded that police archives 'have often been neglected and vast amounts of material has been destroyed or taken to decorate someone's book shelf.' The Forward to the survey was written by Lord Knights, ex-Chief Constable and then President of the Police History Society. He called for police forces to adopt 'a coherent archive policy dealing with the criteria for selective weeding and the support system necessary for police records as a whole.'[10] In 1992, the Police History Society produced and distributed a pamphlet for police forces on the best way to set up a records management policy.[11] Action was taken by a few forces who founded museums and appointed archivists. But while some new documentation has come to light in the years after the 1989 survey, some of the catalogued documents have subsequently disappeared.[12] Some of the museums have also gone: the document holdings of Cambridgeshire's closed museum went to the county record office, the artefacts went somewhere else.

The present survey was intended to test whether or not Lord Knights's plea had been noted and acted upon in the intervening 13 years. Its methodology was extremely crude. In late March 2003 a circular letter was sent out to the chief officers and chairs of police authorities of all the provincial forces in Britain outside London. The response rate to our enquiry was as follows:

Table One: Response Rate

	Total	Responses	%
GB	49	29	59
England	37	21	57
Wales	4	2	50
Scotland	8	6	75

We asked:
1. What is your force's policy for archiving its records for future research access?
2. What is your force's policy for controlling access to these records?
3. Do you have any contact with the local Record Office?

4. Is there an officer or staff member in your force with specific responsibility for archive policy?
5. Do you consider that the implementation of the 2000 Freedom of Information Act and the recommendations of the government's 'e-envoy' regarding the archiving of electronic information will change the way your force deals with these issues?

We might assume that the forces who did not respond would include all of those who place little priority on access to their records by historians. But we would be wrong: the non-respondents included at least one force that we know has a very restrictive policy but also at least one other that has an active museum and a good archive policy.

Several forces referred us to the Association of Chief Police Officers – ACPO – who are coordinating a project to develop procedures for police forces to implement Freedom of Information legislation.[13] ACPO have written a draft set of procedures which they published in 2003 as an internal consultation document.[14] A similar process is going on north of the border in order to comply with the 2002 Freedom of Information (Scotland) Act, but the Association of Chief Police Officers Scotland have yet to arrive at a final draft.[15]

The answers we got showed that the five questions asked were more ambiguous than we had hoped. For example, many forces had very different views of what constituted an archiving policy: some saw this as pertaining only to 'old' records, some only to those still in regular use and others saw it as an ongoing process involving the selection and retention of records. In order to reach conclusions about the issues that interested us, we needed to analyse the responses further to get an idea of the key issues that the responses revealed. In some cases the responses were explicitly stated; in others they became apparent from the answers given by the forces concerned to our original questions.[16]

Table Two: Interpretative summary of answers regarding key issues

	No.	% of responses
Does the force appear to only be thinking about the use of records for operational reasons?	10	36
Any contact with a record office?	13	46

Is there an internal force museum of any kind?	6	21
Does there appear to be provision for ongoing archiving of material as it becomes useless for operational purposes?	10	36
Is there an appreciation of the wide variety of material that will be of interest to future historians?	3	10
Has the force realised that the preservation of electronic records involves a whole new series of challenges?	1	4

Just over a third of the forces that responded appeared to consider records only in terms of management and operational material, and thus chose to interpret the question about 'future research access' as referring essentially to sociological, rather than historical research. Records were there to be kept for a few years – generally between three and 25, depending on the status of the document.

Just under half had had some kind of contact with a local record office for the purposes of records deposit. This does not necessarily mean that all was well: one force claimed that:

> Our local Record Office are occasionally contacted to see if they are interested in any documents due for disposal. This is a rare occurrence. I spoke to the local office and they pointed out that much of what is of interest to them is in the public domain anyway.[17]

Six forces had their own museums or museum collections, or were in contact with local museums, but all but one of these were also in contact with record offices. Most museums were minor affairs, although at least one of the forces which responded employs a full-time curator. Others have an active voluntary curator or an interested group of retired police officers who appear to do this job properly.

An overt resistance to research was present in some responses. On the issue of policy, one respondent wrote that 'We do not necessarily interpret "research" as a "need to know".'[18] Some responses also demonstrated a willingness to close a wide range of 'sensitive' documents: though to be fair, these came from forces that had at least preserved and archived documents and worked out a policy of access to them. Nevertheless, this approach produces the possibly misleading effect (common also in the case of secret or embarrassing central government activities and their attendant records) of creating an impression that things can only get better. When the anodyne and laudatory is available instantly, the organisational machinations appear after 30 years, and the skeletons fall from the cupboard after 75 or more, the image as recorded by historians for the public is one of ever-more benign activity by government agencies. This may or may not be true.

The most important finding is probably the question of ongoing archiving. Only about a third had archive policies that made provision for weeding and preservation of items of historical interest, for indefinite retention. Four forces which had donated 'historical' material to record offices, and thus were obviously aware that they possessed material of historical significance, did not have a procedure for dealing with the material they were generating. A further complicating factor for a decent archiving policy is the semi-autonomous nature of many departments within police forces. Four forces stated that it was departments, rather than the force as a whole, who 'owned' documents and could control access and disposal policies. The closer the 'owner' of the document is to the day-to-day priorities of operational policing, the more difficult it inevitably becomes to give due consideration to priorities whose effects will not be felt for years or even decades.

If we are to be able to write any but the most narrowly administrative history of the British police we need to look beyond minutes of meetings or sources designed for immediate public consumption. Instead, this history has to be worked out from other sources, such as notebooks, refused charge sheets, station incident books, and internal investigations. This is all the more true for the use of police records to examine other social issues historically: the treatment of prostitution, white-collar crime, and traffic policing are just a few that spring to mind. To take one example, the Old Bailey Sessions Papers, now online, are a wonderful source for the study of eighteenth-century social history.[19] From our responses three forces appear to have understood that that 'boring' documents need to be archived too. One force declared that it had no policy for archiving its records for future research access, but drew attention to the fact that it kept Chief Constable's Annual Report and files relating to 'incidents which may be of an historical interest'.[20] Police Annual Reports are glossy and Panglossian publications, designed to show the force in the best light possible.

The final interesting issue is whether they appreciate the forthcoming problems for permanent storage that might be caused by the increased use of electronic access. Twenty-seven did not list this in their expected impacts of the move towards e-government. The exception was one Scottish force, whose archivist has also noted that the different provisions of the Scottish and English/Welsh Freedom of Information Acts means that certain categories of UK-wide information might be open one side of the border but not the other.

Almost all police forces do appreciate the likely impact of the Freedom of Information Acts, and it is this that is driving them to adopt a unified records management strategy for the first time. This will of necessity incorporate some degree of public access. However, given the real need for security, the demands of confidentiality, and attitudes displayed in the survey responses, notably the absolute priority often given to operational use of information, there is a chance that the guidelines might make things worse. What we need to do, therefore, is make sure that when the guidelines are finalised, a role for the preservation of all kinds of records – sensitive or not – for future historians is written in. Long delays in access might even be preferable if the alternative was the *status quo*, which in too many cases is complete destruction. We need a levelling-up to the practices of the best forces, rather than levelling-down to those of the worst.

In conclusion, we heard enough encouraging noises in these responses to feel slightly less despondent about the state of the British provincial police service as a subject for future study. Most police records continue to be consigned to a locked filing cabinet, or destroyed outright with no thought for the needs of posterity, but in a few forces a more enlightened attitude prevails. For most of the forces there is a lot more that needs to be done, and until it is, the provincial police of Britain will continue to be overshadowed in the historical record by the Metropolitan Police and by the intelligence services. With luck, academic conclusions ought to feed though to the public debate: but in a wider and more direct sense, an open government, where information is a resource that can be directly accessed by as many people as possible, underpinned by cultures of institutional openness limited only by the prevention of harm, is a step on the way to a more open and healthy society.

Notes

1. C. Emsley, 'The Archives of the English and Welsh Police forces: A Survey' in L.A. Knafla and S.W.S. Binney (eds.) *Law, Society and the State: Essays in Modern Legal History* (Toronto: University of Toronto Press, 1995), pp. 465–476, 465–466.
2. Emsley 'Archives', pp. 468–469.
3. Local Government Act, 1972, (c. 70).
4. C. Emsley, *The English Police, a Social and Political History* (London: Longman, 1996), pp. 162–5.
5. Criminal Procedure and Investigations Act 1996 (c.25).
6. M. Young, *An Inside Job: Policing and Police Culture in Britain* (Oxford: Clarendon Press, 1991), p. 35.
7. For example, ACPO guidelines on media relations state that: 'As a publicly accountable body, the Police Service is committed to openness and accessibility'; ACPO Guidelines, December 2000. Metropolitan Police Commissioner Paul Condon pledged to 'to encourage openness, understanding, and trust' in 1998; 'Building an anti-racist Metropolitan Police Service' MPS press release, 1 October 1998.
8. H. Beynon, 'Regulating Research: Politics and Decision making in industrial organisations' in A. Bryman (ed.) *Doing Research in Organizations* (London: Routledge, 1988) pp. 21–33, p. 23; Young, *Inside Job*, p. 29.
9. Sir Robert Mark called his memoirs 'In the Office of Constable'. R Mark, *In the Office of Constable* (London: Collins, 1978). The most explicit historical hagiographies of the British police were written by Charles Reith, e.g. C. Reith, *British Police and the Democratic Ideal* (London: Oxford University Press, 1943), but many more recent and popular historians have taken up his themes, e.g. D. Ascoli, *The Queen's Peace: the origins and development of the Metropolitan Police, 1829–1979* (London: Hamish Hamilton, 1979).
10. I Bridgeman and C. Emsley, *A guide to the archives of the police forces of England and Wales* (Cambridge: Police History Society, 1989).
11. L.A. Waters, *Towards a Record Management Policy for Provincial Police Forces in England and Wales*. (Cambridge: Police History Society 1992).
12. Emsley 'Archives', 468.
13. Freedom of Information Act 2000 (c. 36).
14. Personal communication, 11 June 2003 from ACPO representative.
15. Freedom of Information (Scotland) Act 2002 (asp. 13).
16. NB: Responses are out of 28 because no final return was received from one force owing to a failure to respond to their request for clarification.
17. Response from force number 5.
18. Response from force number 1.
19. http://www.oldbaileyonline.org/
20. Response from force number 23.

Chapter Five

History for Sale? The Battle to Preserve Britain's Fire History[1]

Shane Ewen

In the future the history of Britain's fire and rescue services might only be available to those prepared to pay to access the relevant documents. As part of the New Labour government's proposed reform agenda for Britain's fire and rescue service, fire and rescue authorities will be empowered to charge users for particular services. Since the Fire Service Act, 1947, fire authorities have been entitled to charge for any call-out to a non-fire-fighting special service incident (SSI).[2] The proposals, if put into effect, will empower fire authorities to levy a charge for SSIs without receiving consent and also to charge a third party for a service provided to others. Authorities will also be entitled to charge for non-SSIs, including the loan of equipment for public displays, the provision or removal of water, training and consultancy work, and the supply of documents. The latter will encompass the provision of fire scene photographs and video footage, copies of fire reports and the issue of fire certificates. It is proposed that 'any person, company or organisation requesting the supply of this category of service' will be liable to face a charge for the supply of documents.[3]

On first reading this might appear reasonable to academics and enthusiasts with an interest in the service and an appreciation of the financial pressures in the wake of the national fire strike and pay deal in 2002–03.⁴ The proposals also confirm that requests for documents made under the Data Protection Act 1998, will be protected. Moreover it is 'expected' that access to historical records will be protected by the Freedom of Information Act 2000, although availability 'would be at the discretion of each individual Fire Authority and also whether the supply of this documentation would be subject to a fee.' Archiving such material would remain a decision for individual local authorities under the Local Government Act 1972.⁵

Leaving the retention, storage and charging of historical documents to the discretion of fire authorities under intense political and financial pressure sets a dangerous precedent which other public sector services might follow. There are already concerns that the Home Office might follow the Office of the Deputy Prime Minister's example in regionalising service delivery within the police, which could have a destabilising impact on existing police museums as resources are increasingly concentrated. Although fire-fighters are generally knowledgeable of their service history, there are concerns that senior management and policy-makers lack appreciation of the value of records for historical study. Fire certificates, for example, shed light on the shifting attitudes of authorities towards fire prevention since their inception in 1971 and are a valuable source for analysing health and safety in the workplace, while photographs and videos provide a firsthand account of incidents that might otherwise be confined to secondary accounts in incident books and the media.⁶ Yet the government has drawn up the battle-ground by making them subject to charging.

Preserving the past
The police historian is aware of the value of fire records for enhancing the history of individual forces and the development of professional values within criminal justice and local government. With a large proportion of fire brigades managed by police forces between the mid-nineteenth-century and 1941 when they were abolished, the provincial police played a crucial role in the development of fire-fighting administrative and operational standards. Both services also provide a window onto the development of public services and both share common characteristics in terms of their working cultures, hierarchical struc-

tures and gendered divisions. Changing access to fire records, therefore, has direct relevance to the police historian's research. Indeed the preservation of fire service history is like that of the police, being centred on an interdependent institutional framework consisting of archive repositories, preservation groups and museums. This paper will briefly outline how each structure within this framework operates before discussing how recent attempts have been made to facilitate greater integration to promote the preservation of fire history.

(i) Fire archives
The first place any historian must begin in researching fire history is in a local authority archive. Like other public records, the quality and quantity of the available documents varies according to local archival policies and fire authority records management strategies. Indeed, local government reorganisation in the mid-1970s meant that many local records were 'lost' or 'consolidated'. Committee minute books, annual reports and incident books are available for most brigades, but it is more difficult to trace other records that shed light on the working structures and cultures of local brigades, notably personnel files.[7]

There is no national fire service archive. The National Archives holds records for the administration of the service by central government departments, which from the 1920s until 2001 was chiefly the responsibility of the Home Office. Records relating to fire protection during the Second World War are common, although there is a paucity of records for the decades before the 1920s, which reflects the diverse nature of fire protection before then.[8] Elsewhere most professional associations hold their own archives (including the Institution of Fire Engineers, the Fire Protection Association and the British Fire Service Association) which are accessible by appointment only. Other archives, including those of local private fire brigade associations, are often retained by individual members and can be difficult to access.[9]

The Fire Service College is Britain's national training college for fire-fighters, specialising in fire safety and engineering. The College Library holds the most comprehensive collection of fire safety and emergency response literature in the world. Having obtained a grant from the Fire Service Research and Training Trust in 2001,[10] the Library opened an archive in 2002 maintained to the prescribed standards recommended by the National Archives under the

Public Records Act 1959. In 1998 the College appointed an honorary archivist with responsibility for cataloguing the Library's collections. However, the archive is far from a national collection, and visions of a truly national fire archive remain a distant reality as a shifting focus within the service towards risk assessment and integrated personal development systems (IPDS) accounts for an increasing proportion of the College's resources.[11] However, the College archivist has performed an important co-ordinating role within the fire community and is fostering links with government agencies, museums, archives and preservation groups with a view to creating a UK Fire Historical Society and a sound archive collection in conjunction with the Imperial War Museum.[12]

(ii) Preservation groups and collectors

Enthusiasts are the lifeblood of fire history. Not all are serving or retired firefighters, although most have some connection with the service. Enthusiasts play an undeniably central role in recording and preserving the past. Often originating locally, preservation groups are voluntary organisations that restore old appliances and collect memorabilia relating to fire history in their localities. Funds are secured through membership costs, fund-raising activities, and grants or other assistance (such as storage facilities) from local authorities. The Fire Service Preservation Group (founded in 1968) is the largest of these organisations with branches throughout the country, and insures its members to the sum of £2 million for the display and use of their equipment at exhibitions and public rallies. Meanwhile, fire service medal and uniform collectors, whilst a constant source of irritation to some (especially those bombarded with requests for information on medal recipients), are a useful repository of knowledge to those with an interest in overlapping themes such as discipline and masculinity.

The Fire Brigade Society (founded in 1963) provides a national forum for enthusiasts interested in fire history and preservation. As part of its activities it employs a fleet historian who is responsible for creating a national fleet database consisting of all pre- and post-1974 appliances. More recently attempts have been made to create a fire station history archive, including data on each individual station's location and operational status as well as opening and closure dates. Clearly the success of such ventures is dependent on the enthusiasm of committed members, and the death of one member can lead to some features of its work lying dormant.[13]

(iii) Museums

Since the late 1970s there have been concerted moves to establish a national fire museum by the Fire Services National Museum Trust (FSNMT), a small group of enthusiasts and serving and retired fire-fighters. The chief objective of the FSNMT is to educate the public about the dangers of fire, but it is also committed to the collection and preservation of vehicles, documents and artefacts of historic importance, while acting as a hub for the dissemination of information amongst local museums and preservation groups. The FSNMT has, however, faced many difficulties, not least in, firstly, finding a suitable location for the museum and, secondly, obtaining planning permission to convert a listed building at Weedon in Northamptonshire for use as a museum. Attracting significant funds to restore the building is the latest difficulty facing the Trustees.[14]

Yet Britain lags behind North America and Europe in the creation of uniform standards for establishing and managing fire museums and the fostering of close networks between stakeholders. The Fire Museum Network (FMN), for example, was formed in 1995 after six years of seminars held under the auspices of the International Association of Fire Chiefs. By serving as a clearing house for information and co-ordinating networking activities for more than 200 museums in North America, the FMN has continued to organise seminars and has promoted the adoption of uniform standards in the collection, preservation and display of artefacts. Meanwhile the Comité Technique International de Prévention et d'Extinction du Feu (CTIF) (founded in 1900), which promotes fire prevention internationally, held an international conference for fire service historians in 1992, from which a study group was formed, culminating in the formation of a CTIF Commission for History, Museums and Documentation in 1998. Although this venture was chiefly initiated to celebrate the CTIF's centenary, that it was deemed appropriate to establish a separate Commission alongside others responsible for technical issues, such as hazardous materials, airport protection and forest fires, indicates the importance attached to fire heritage on the continent. The publication of standard procedures for fire museums and 'tradition rooms' within stations has underlined the importance of the service's history and the dissemination of information on collective traditions.[15]

Notwithstanding the problems encountered by the FSNMT and the pressures on local museums, there has been a recent resurgence in national activity to promote fire history and encourage fire authorities and other organisations to invest in the preservation and display of their heritage. In October 2003 Britain's first fire museum seminar was held under the auspices of the Greater Manchester Fire Service Museum (GMFSM), one of the few successful local fire museums. Chaired by the GMFSM's curator, Divisional Officer Bob Bonner, the seminar attracted 33 delegates from 15 separate organisations involved in the preservation or study of fire heritage. Presentations from representatives of the fire service, local fire museums and the wider heritage sector stressed the importance of establishing a co-ordinated approach to fire history to offset the 'pressures and restraints' on local authorities. Bonner has noted that there has since been an increase in networking amongst museums and a Management Group is planning a second seminar.[16]

This suggests that there is indeed scope for the preservation of the service's rich history, although this remains dependent on the enthusiastic, and invariably voluntary, contribution of individuals, the goodwill of fire authorities to provide storage space for large appliances, and the success of such organisations to raise their profile within the fire service community and, more importantly, the general public. The success of a museum and archive depends on the committed enthusiast for its establishment, but its future is ultimately measured by the level of public usage. Moreover, the threat to introduce charging places fire museums, archives and users in an unstable position. How organisations like the FSNMT and the Management Group of the fire museum seminars progress towards their shared objective of preserving the service's history for the education and entertainment of the public depends on their access to memorabilia in good working order, photographs and other visual records, and written documentation (which has implications for the preservation of electronic records, especially with the government's commitment to the application of e-government within the fire service). Such access, including that of the academic to important records, must surely remain free in order for fire history to flourish as a legitimate subject of study both in its own right and as part of broader research into public services and organisational cultures.

Conclusions

This brief case study supports recent claims that archival policies are subject to political pressures, especially where there is a need to raise additional funding to balance demands for greater investment in heritage with demands for a more efficient use of existing resources.[17] Yet it remains to be seen what impact the introduction of charging for the supply of documents will have on the retention and study of Britain's fire heritage. There are also fears that the proposed reforms could be the first step towards charging museums and preservation groups for their access to obsolescent appliances, equipment and documentation. Moreover, and of greater interest to the historian, charging could seriously impact on studies of fire safety, working practices, organisational cultures and the growth in bureaucratic procedures. This is a backwards step from recent moves to improve government-sponsored research into fire safety and service culture.[18]

Evidently there are common lessons for those interested in criminal justice and fire history, not least the need to convince policy-makers and those responsible for budgets of the benefits of investing in their heritage. These include the fostering of an integrated professional identity and greater social inclusion with an allegedly disinterested public. The preservation of fire heritage also contains an educational element. Attracting school groups and youth organisations to museums gives a fire authority the opportunity to show children the dangers of playing with fire and the irresponsibility of arson, the single biggest cause of fires. It also enables authorities to demonstrate the advances made in fire safety, which are not always clear to the uninitiated. Of course, this is not a new idea. In 1891 the Birmingham fire brigade established a fire museum which included exhibitions of apparatus and working demonstrations of electric lighting and spontaneous combustion to entertain and educate. Funded entirely from the brigade's annual budget, its chief officer, Alfred Tozer, recognised the importance of respectable leisure in fostering civic pride in a local institution during a period of intensive urban development.[19] Modern fire authorities could learn much from their predecessors, especially as the focus shifts from local communities towards regional bureaucracies. The government may win the battle over charging for documents, but they cannot win the war over making fire history accessible to the academic, enthusiast and general public.

Notes

1. The author would like to acknowledge, amongst others, Michael Kernan (Fire Service College Honorary Archivist and Historian), Amanda Collicutt (Fire Service College Library Manager) and David Stevens (former General Secretary to the British Fire Service Association) for their assistance.
2. The government's proposals are outlined in S. Ewen, ' "Our fire and rescue service": a local, regional or national responsibility', *History & Policy*, 20 (2004), accessible at www.historyandpolicy.org/archive/policy-paper-20.html. SSIs include road traffic accidents, cleaning spillages and leaks, rescuing trapped persons, and providing assistance at aircraft and railway incidents.
3. Office of the Deputy Prime Minister, *Charging by Fire and Rescue Authorities: A Consultation Document* (HMSO: London, 2004), pp.11–12.
4. The strike is covered in R. Pyper, 'Fire-fighters' dispute: playing with fire', *Parliamentary Affairs*, LVI (2003), pp.490–505.
5. Personal correspondence from Greg Watt (Fire Service Effectiveness Issues Branch, ODPM), 15 Apr. 2004.
6. The recent release of a video, *Britain's Fire Services at War*, of operational footage from the National Fire Service indicates the value of visual images to the historian.
7. Where these do exist they are incomplete and written permission to view them is often required from the fire authority.
8. S. Ewen, 'Central government and the modernization of the British fire service, 1900–38', *Twentieth Century British History*, XIV, 4 (2003), pp.317–38.
9. A few, like the Coventry and Bedford private fire associations, have been deposited at local archives.
10. The main purpose of the Trust is to fund research into fire safety, but there has recently been an increasing focus on social science research.
11. IPDS involves the creation of a role-based, rather than rank-based, system to provide fire-fighters with a structured career path.
12. Personal correspondence from Michael Kernan, 19 Apr. 2004, 16 Jul. 2004.
13. *Fire Cover*, 155 (2002), p.5.
14. *Fire*, LXXX, 987 (1987), pp.61–2; *Saved: The Magazine of the Friends of the Fire Services National Museum Trust*, 22 (2000), pp.4–6.
15. CTIF, *The History of the International Fire Brigade Council and the CTIF 1900–2000* (CTIF: Nainville les Roches, 2000), pp.137–40.
16. *Fire*, XCVI, 1182 (2003), p.4; *Fire*, XCVII, 1188 (2004), p.6.
17. M. Steemson, 'Political pressure and the archival record', *History & Policy*, 22 (2004), accessible at http://www.historyandpolicy.org/archive/policy-paper-22.html.
18. Office of the Deputy Prime Minister, *Draft Fire and Rescue National Framework* (HMSO: London, 2003), ch. 9.
19. *Fire & Water*, VIII, 93, (1891), pp.139–40.

Chapter Six

A Chance to Find Out

Dave Cross

This chapter is the written version of the short talk that I gave in June 2004, about the main issues facing police and crime museums in the future. It looks at several issues that must be on the agenda for discussion. They include the compatibility of electronic records, the anomalous practices governing disclosure, the potentially injurious impact of the Data Protection and Freedom of Information Acts, and the conflicting demands of research and confidentiality. I have identified some potential ways forward, concerning storage, disclosure, and criteria for future archiving.

When the 'New Police' were formed, in 1829 and the years thereafter, records were mainly kept with ink and paper in thick bound volumes. Every person who wished to apply for a post with the new police completed an examination form; if they were accepted, the form was kept and, in the case of Birmingham Police, bound in a volume. We still have most of these forms. They show where the applicant was born, his age (no date of birth) where he lived, if he was married or single, his trade or profession and a few other details. These forms can, if you are lucky, be found for Warwickshire, Staffordshire, Worcester and no doubt many other areas either with a County Archive or regional museum. At the West Midlands Police Museum, we have Birmingham City Police discipline records up to the 1950s, plus a few from the old West Midlands Constabulary. No old crime reports have been archived. The museum is fortunate to have 5,000 old Victorian and Edwardian prisoner's photographs, each giving the prisoner's details on the same form as the photo.

That is the situation as it now stands, but if we jump forward to the year 2104, what can we anticipate having saved for our children's children? We could be expected to have no excuse not to have made a good job of it, since everything is on now done on computers. But let's look at a possible situation: Museum A has a record of every person who was employed by company C, because the records were donated by a staff member when the company went broke in 2019. They are all on a CD-ROM ... but, (as we've know for a few years) CD-ROMs degenerate. We could have copied them, but we have just too many, and our computer system did not match the system they were written to, so they are lost. Museum B has a record of all soldiers who served in the great conflicts between 1985 and 2004 but again all records are not compatible with any known computer system. The historian who saved them in compressed format on little floppy discs never correctly documented the details of the system which he used to do it.

I myself have matched hundreds of court reports from the newspapers of the day to some of the Victorian prisoners' photographs the West Midlands Police Museum holds. Given how rarely the Victorians had their photographs taken compared to today, these are a rare and precious source. The notes are stored as Word Perfect files, which are not compatible with Microsoft Word. What happens when my old computer breaks down as it must do sooner or later? This is a problem that we are facing now; one created over a period little more than ten years, and just one aspect of the problem of compatibility and durability of electronic records.

We have seen several different storage systems come onto the scene; from fifteen inch floppy discs to five and quarter inch floppy discs to three inch floppy discs, then CD-ROMS, DVDs, and digital storage. All these media need some form of technical retrieval system; systems that change rapidly over time. We know that paper archives, when properly stored, can be preserved, but the logistics of storing the volumes of paper such as are currently being produced are daunting. Can we help to solve this problem of storage using old technology?

We have been using 70mm, 35mm, and 16mm film strip for nearly 100 years. Modern film is quite stable, viewers are simple to operate and no doubt there will be a system that I can buy for £35 in a few years time in order to read these archives on my wireless computer. Maybe this is the answer to problems that electronic records have with durability and readability.

There are more issues that confront us. One is the problem of disclosure rules. An archive might answer, in response to an enquiry, that all its records are closed for fifty years. Another, twenty-five years. But when does this count start? From the date that the records were deposited, from the date of the last entry, from the date of the death of the subject of the records, or from the date written on them? Often this is subject to the discretion and interpretation of a committee. I am at a loss to give a consistent explanation for the rules; most appear to be highly subject to local variations.

Obviously, police personnel records should be considered confidential by default. We apply the following rules at the West Midlands Police Museum. As a rule of thumb, the records of officers who were born less than 75 years before the date of the request should not be available. Unless known otherwise, it must be assumed the officer or his wife are still alive. If the person making the request is asking about their father or grandfather, then they ought to be able to furnish proof that both the officer and his wife are deceased. But if not, the museum needs to inquire about the sons and or daughters of the officer: are they still alive; would they object to the enquirer obtaining information? If on the date of enquiry the officer would be over 100, then it is safe to assume that both he and his wife are deceased, but again information ought only to be available to immediate members of the family. Should an enquiry be received from a member of the public about a specific officer that person is not related to, then access should not be readily available.

Students researching through colleges or universities are required to provide confirmation of their course, and a supporting letter from the tutor. In cases of this nature, no officers are to be named in their notes, as the research is limited to the officer's role and service in the police as opposed to personal and disciplinary information. One example of the way this has worked in practice is a recent project looking at why so many officers joined or rejoined the police after the Second World War, and then left within months. For example, in one entry of 30 officers joining, only three stayed longer than 12 months. No officers were named in the output, but this was nevertheless important research, carried out on records which would normally be closed.

Another potential pitfall concerns the Data Protection and Freedom of Information Acts. I will not talk about them in detail here. But if I were a gambling man, I would suggest that some members of senior management – in whatever industry you wish to think of – are saying, 'If we haven't kept any records, and have a short archiving period, then our potential expenses and liability on this subject will be limited.' This state of affairs is likely to lead to more records being lost. Even archiving with close reference to compliance with the Data Protection Act can cause problems. There comes time when a specific part of that record ceases to be covered by the Act, but since the record, possibly updated on many occasions, is kept amongst other records that are still covered by it, the records as a whole are not suitable for depositing in any public archive. Therefore they are more likely to be destroyed than archived. Or take the case of Bill, a 68-year-old Korean War veteran. Bill took early retirement a few years ago and sat down to work on his hobby: tracing all the people who served with him in Korea; their names, regiments and awards. The list runs into thousands of ex-servicemen. Does he realise that this record could be, and probably is, subject to the Data Protection Act? We have to wonder whether or not this was what the Act was really intended for.

What, then, needs to be archived? Obviously items of great national importance, such as the Churchill Papers. From a the point of view of police, and of the Police History Society, obviously we need to keep personnel records for police officers and nowadays also for the increasing number of civilian support staff. Will students and genealogists in 2104 want to know how we did the job in 2004? I seriously believe they will, probably to a greater extent than do the students of 2004. We must at least give them a chance to find out. Modern policing rests on the basis of crime reports and crime analysis systems. To date none that I know to are archived, yet in 100 years time, how interesting will these files be to the trainee criminologist? At this stage we cannot know how interesting, but again, above all we have to give them a chance to find out. And if given access to a run of twenty years of complete crime records, will the trainee criminologist of 2020 be able to develop new and better systems for their community? They too should at least be given the chance to find out.

I would not deem to try to answer the question of 'how to archive' in its entirety. But we have a responsibility to leave records for our descendants so they can carry out research, whether as pensioners or students. It is not my position to suggest a national system both for what and how we archive, but as museums officer for the Police History Society, I can only ask that the least we can do is to give them a chance to find out.

CONFIDENTIAL.
Police Information No. 2240.
Telephone Nos. 13—14.

Chief Constable's Office,
Blackpool,
13th June, 1932.

£100 REWARD

Stolen by means of housebreaking in this Borough between 7-40 p.m. and 10-10 p.m., Friday, 10th June, 1932. Entrance effected by forcing window at rear and climbing through.

BRACELET.	Lady's Gold Expanding Bracelet, diamond in centre surrounded by diamonds, with diamonds extending half way around the Bracelet. Valued £400.
RING.	Lady's Single Stone Diamond Ring, all platinum mounts, claw set, between 3 and 4 carat. Valued £450.
WRISTLET WATCH.	Lady's Platinum Wristlet Watch, about size of shilling, surrounded by 29 diamonds, attached to a Silver Bangle. No. of Watch 272655. Valued £100.
BROOCH.	Gold Bar Brooch with aquamarine in centre. Valued £5.
BROOCH.	Pearl Pear-shaped Brooch, filigree. Valued £5.
EAR-RINGS.	Pair of Ear-rings, pearl and aquamarine. Valued £5.
BROOCH. EAR-RINGS.	Gold Cameo Brooch, female head in pink and white, with Gold and Cameo Ear-rings to match. Valued £8.
FINGER WATCH.	Lady's Gold Ring with small oval-shaped watch in face, silver dial. Valued £12.
MESH BAG.	Gold Mesh Bag, 7ins. square, the clip set with black stone.
PENDANT CHAIN.	Antique Pendant, pear-shaped topaz drop, lemon coloured stone, rather large size, attached to silver chain, filigree pattern. Valued £25.
PENDANT.	Gold and Pearl Filigree Pendant. Valued £10.

A reward of £100 or pro rata of the value of property recovered is offered by Messrs. Marcus Fleeson & Co., 9, Albert Square, Manchester, Assessors, for information leading to the recovery of the above-described jewellery, and the apprehension of the offender.

Please cause enquiries to be made at Pawnbrokers and Jewellers with a view to tracing the property described herein and any information received kindly communicate with the undersigned, or to any Police Station.

H. E. DERHAM,
Chief Constable.

Poster issued by the Chief Constable of Blackpool in 1932, now in the police archive at the Open University

Part Three

Ways Forward

Chapter Seven

Museum Status, Storage Demands and 'Hearts and Minds': Three Insurmountable Areas?

Charles Griffiths

To those who have considered such matters, the conclusion may be reached that it is curious that many of our towns and cities will have a museum dedicated to its local or county military unit; the South Wales Borderers in Brecon, Gordon Highlanders in Aberdeen and The King's Regiment in Liverpool, to name just three examples out of hundreds. There are also many museums covering just about every other aspect of our heritage; but it may be thought rather peculiar that those dedicated to our old Borough and County Police Forces are perilously thin on the ground.

One reason for this apparent anomaly may be put down to lack of 'corporate pride'. If we look at Regimental Museums for example, it can be found that most old soldiers have proudly extolled their regiment at great length and contributed in some way towards their museum; but to many police officers – both past and present – their particular force was/is little more than a steady job with a pension at the end. While this may or may not be entirely true, there certainly is evidence to suggest that there was much more pride in, and loyalty shown to, local forces in the days before the great amalgamations of 1947 and 1968 – something that also happens to ring true with regard to military organisations, although to a much lesser extent. However, this only partly explains why there are so few police museums.

After three major wars and countless smaller campaigns in the last century, there has been no shortage of benefactors willing to contribute to the memory of fallen sons and their regiments, with the result that, in general, military barracks have usually been able to find room for some form of museum; and service personnel, along with strong Regimental Associations, have ever been willing to find ways of raising money for their needs. That is not to say that police have never been up to the challenge of fund-raising; indeed, they have shown themselves to be perfectly capable of raising substantial funds for a broad range of charities – but rarely for their own museum. If we overlook the initial 'lack of pride' syndrome, there are in fact three sound reasons why police museums never quite get off the ground in the UK – the first, and probably most important of all is the failure to win hearts and minds.

The winning of hearts and minds
From the outset, there has to be a 'will from above', for unless the Commissioner or Chief Constable offers full approval and sanction, all plans for a museum will fall at this first hurdle. Since each UK-based police force is part-financed by the local community it serves, the Chief has to balance the needs of the museum against the use of public funds; is the (usually) inadequate budget to be spent on extra police officers and equipment, or on preserving the force history? In most chief officers' minds – quite understandably – there is no room for debate! But that is not to say that he or she cannot be won over. If the need for a museum can be shown, there is little reason – other than funding – why approval and support cannot be achieved at this stage; and if a museum is to be initiated, both of the latter will be essential.

If the Chief's approval can be obtained, it may only be forthcoming on the basis of raising substantial funds. There are probably countless means of achieving a proportion of the amount necessary. But here we meet another obstacle. As noted earlier, officers are generally willing to engage in all manner of activities in order to raise money for charity, but, by and large, they tend to give little thought to their own history – their *raison d'être* more likely being their job in hand – and asking them to fundraise for something of little interest to them is almost certain to meet with a less than enthusiastic response. On the other hand, and in general, support staff and even the most senior officers will often enter into the spirit of fund-raising on a very different level, frequently with outstanding results.

Seeking support for a museum from different departments invariably requires inventive approaches, but it does appear that the more one can encourage each department to contribute items of historical interest, the more responsive they become to the idea of having a museum; and involving individuals does seem to engender a sense of pride, especially when some of those individuals have had a personal connection or recollection of a particular item during its last useful contribution – such items frequently lurking hidden and forgotten in some dark corner. Suitably enthused and involved, departments may even be further encouraged to sponsor a display or contribute towards the cost of 'their own' particular item's conservation. Unfortunately, what funds that might be raised are unlikely to be enough to cover the costs of one minor museum project, let alone the initial set-up costs of the museum itself. Nevertheless, their collective interest, enthusiasm, involvement and support are vital in taking you towards your objective.

Thus far, our hearts and minds approach has been directed internally; there is yet the important matter of winning over the general public who, after all, will be the main beneficiaries. The means of achieving public interest and support are wide and varied, necessitating the use of newspaper and other media coverage, contacting businesses and organisations, seeking sponsorship, giving talks to interested societies and so on; the list of ways and means is limitless. With properly directed effort, the problems of funding can eventually be overcome – but not unless that initial battle of hearts and minds has been won! Should that battle be overcome – bearing in mind that it is never-ending – there is then the second obstacle to be met, concerning storage and preservation.

The demands of storage
Probably as a result of a combination of lack of pride, shortage of will, poor

resources and across-the-board destruction policies, UK police forces have never been very good at retaining their heritage. If this were not bad enough, those exceptional forces that did manage in the past to keep hold of a few artefacts and memorabilia, kept them more often than not in the wholly inadequate storerooms of old, damp and musty Victorian stations. Here, much of what had been kept away from the public at large, slowly but inevitably disintegrated under unsuitable conditions and neglect. Only in the last thirty or so years has this changed with the building of more modern stations and a resurgence of interest in family and local history.

In spite of this, it seems that, by design, modern stations and headquarters buildings have not been graced with an excess of storage space – a situation with which many officers and staff will be familiar. The old coalhouses, outhouses and bunkers have largely all gone, but they have not been replaced with any other means of storage. I have used the word 'storage' as a coverall, for of necessity, museums require considerable space for three essential areas: general storage, conservation and display. If one adds to these an archive and curator's office along with the accoutrements necessary to do the job, the difficulty of finding sufficient space is hugely increased. Regrettably, very few police forces have the privilege of providing such extravagant areas, and consequently, space remains at a premium.

Unlike the private collector who somehow manages to create his or her own little home display, corporate museums cannot keep their artefacts in any old cupboards and drawers. As specialist repositories, they have an obligation to ensure that their collection is properly conserved for the benefit of everyone. This necessitates the use of highly expensive and specialist conservation, cleaning and storage materials, thermographic, ultra-violet, insect and security controls, plus the usual modern-day office equipment – all of which adds up to a complete department in its own right – a department generally unconnected with normal day-to-day police business, and as such, not high on the agenda of police priorities. Unfortunately, without these necessary materials and, from the outset, the requisite storage space required to house them, there will be no opportunity to advance to the third problem stage: registering as an official museum.

Attaining museum status

Here I would reiterate the word used earlier: 'obligation'. In maintaining the heritage of the community it serves, every museum has – or should have – an obligation or onus of responsibility enshrined in its constitution to ensure that its collection is properly cared for, and that obligation must be impressed upon, and taken into account by our police chiefs, police authorities and everyone else who has a direct input into the running of the museum. To this end, there are certain standards and criteria that the museum must meet.

Working towards those standards is extremely labour-intensive, time-consuming and costly. Meeting the demands of storage is only one important factor. In order to gain recognised status, the museum must have a legal, constitutional document specifying ownership, a charitable or other recognised status, a defined purpose, an acquisition and disposal policy and working practice, and it must conform to the various legislation regarding public access, disabled access, discrimination, health and safety, opening times, admission charges etc – many of these happily falling within standard police policies. To these may be added specialist insurance for storage, display and transit, fire exits, security arrangements, code of practice and much more besides. Only when these elements have been fully incorporated into the museum constitution – which must proceed through the legal channels for general acceptance, then onward to the Chief and Police Authority for sanction – is the end document acceptable to the current body responsible for regulating museum registration. This has been variously known as 'Museums and Galleries Commission', 'Resource', and at the time of writing is represented regionally by 'Museums, Libraries and Archives Councils' – the name changes with monotonous regularity!

It should be understood that Registered Museum Status cannot and will not be granted unless the museum conforms to the basic requirements as referred to above. Without proper storage, display and access facilities, or initial funding, you will be ineligible for grants; without grants it is all but impossible to fund the resources necessary to get started. It is, in other words, a classic chicken-and-egg scenario, and for this reason, the first objective must be to win the hearts and minds of officers, staff and the public at large.

Back to basics

How else then, do we overcome these seemingly insurmountable problem areas? In this writer's view, we really must get back to basics. It is too late to save the police heritage that has already been lost or destroyed, but it is not too late to preserve what we already have. Both at local and national levels, we need to take a leaf out of the armed services' book and make each force history a necessary part of the recruit's training curriculum, for without a history, there is no *esprit de corps*; with no *esprit de corps*, there is little pride; and with little pride, there can be no desire for a museum. Once some pride in the force history has been instilled into the recruit's mind, the basic foundation for further building is then in place.

To give an example: I recall that, as a young RUC officer in the 1960s, our force history was a well-established, initial and recurring theme throughout every officer's training, and provided an aspirational standard that never wavered. Throughout my training and subsequent service, I met very few officers who did not harbour some degree of pride in the force. That sense of pride, first established in the days of the old RIC before 1922, was enough to get a force museum started at the outset, and although beset with the usual problems of funding and resources, was nevertheless well supported by successive police hierarchy and force members.

If members of the old UK borough and county police forces ever had a sense of pride in their local force – and there is no reason to suppose they did not – almost certainly it was all lost following amalgamations, as referred to earlier. Excellent examples of this are very much in evidence today in the writer's area of West Wales, where surviving old members of the Pembrokeshire, Cardiganshire and Carmarthenshire Constabularies – to name just three – still refer to the disappointment they felt following amalgamation. To this day, many of them refuse to allow their old uniforms or accoutrements to be retained within what is now Dyfed-Powys Police area, which they see as not being representative of their old force. Since Dyfed-Powys Police incorporates a total of nineteen old borough and county constabularies, it can therefore be seen how easily the cumulative effect of loss of identity and diminished loyalty has brought about our inevitable loss of heritage. By extension, it is probably safe to assume that the same applies throughout the country. With further nationwide amalgamations expected in the future, what little force pride that currently exists will doubtless be further eroded. It is therefore becoming increasingly important to ensure that those police museums that may be in storage, in embryonic form or enjoying some degree of public recognition, find a way of retaining and preserving what heritage they have, otherwise valuable collections could be lost forever!

Unfortunately, precious few police forces can afford the services of a professional curator, let alone the requisite facilities for a proper museum. In many instances, the only acceptable form of museum management is through the services of an 'interested' retired officer or civilian volunteer – the majority of whom having no curatorial or conservational expertise. While we depend on these volunteers, we must at the same time ensure that they have the necessary support and guidance on caring for their collections, otherwise they can do more harm than good. At the earliest possible moment, those forces that do have a collection of sorts should first seek out the conservator in their local County Museum. All artefacts (as indeed all archive materials) degrade with the passage of time, inadequate storage conditions and inexperienced handling; therefore the (usually free) advice of a conservator should be considered a priority.

For those forces wishing to set up a dedicated museum, the table that follows should offer an initial, basic, step-by-step guide in how to progress, although there is no hard and fast rule, and much will depend on the degree of support and funding you can enlist from the chiefs, rank and file and the public in general. To sum up, if we are to avoid losing our local police heritage, we must not make the mistakes of those individuals or forces that, in the past, failed to win hearts and minds, failed the demands of storage and failed to obtain museum status. Make no mistake; each of these difficult problem areas requires enormous dedication, unshakeable tenacity and unstinting willingness if they are to be surmounted. To fail on any one, is to fail on them all, and with that failure comes irretrievable loss.

For further information and guidance on museums and collections, it is worth contacting the Museums, Libraries and Archives Council. Their Website address is: www.mla.gov.uk

Appendix: Setting up a dedicated museum

Step 1	Artefacts	Invite your local conservator to view the collection. Listen to their recommendations.
Step 2	Cleaning	Clean nothing without conservational advice; you may cause irreparable damage.
Step 3	Storage	Obtain at least one room where collection can be held securely and safely. Ensure that all artefacts are kept in stable conditions, and act on professional advice.
Step 4	Authority	Seek authority from the Chief to progress. Enlist his/her support. Impress onus of responsibility.
Step 5	Support	Visit all departments for their support. Acquire forgotten artefacts. Show enthusiasm.
Step5	Funding	Give internal and external talks to all kinds of groups, including council, media and businesses.
Step 6	Status	Contact the funding council (MLA) for their advice, requirements and guidelines, including grants.
Step 7	Display	Give displays where possible, but ensure the collection's security and safety.
Step 8	Constitution	Set up your constitutional documentation outlining ownership, status, A&D policy, working policy, access and display arrangements, committee, etc. Both MLA and local museum can give guidance. From this point you may then be in a position to seek grant aid from Heritage Lottery Fund, and grants from the local council and elsewhere.

Chapter Eight

The Galleries of Justice, Nottingham

Bev Baker

The Galleries of Justice is an independent museum whose three main aims are: to make a difference through our educational work; to collect artefacts, costume and archives which illustrate the history of policing, prisons, the law and the development of the probation service; and thirdly to preserve the building (the Shire Hall, County Gaol, and Police Station) and its history. Through the uniqueness of the building, our collections and the use of costumed interpreters we educate young people and the wider community about crime, citizenship and the law.

The Shire Hall
The Galleries of Justice, Museum of Law, is based at Nottingham's 'Grade Two-star' listed Shire Hall in the heart of the city's historic Lace Market. The Shire Hall has been an important legal and political stronghold, with Assize Courts and Quarter Sessions held here since 1375. There has been a court on the site since 1375 and a prison since as early as 1449. For centuries the Shire Hall was the seat of the King's power in Nottinghamshire. Four times a year, local Justices of the Peace tried people at the Quarter Sessions, while twice a year, the royal judges arrived for the Assizes. The judges were representatives of the

King, and even into the 20th century, their arrival in the town was a scene of medieval pageantry. For the Special Assize in January 1832, following the Reform Bill riots in Nottingham; the judges were met south of Trent Bridge by the High Sheriff of Nottinghamshire with his javelin men and bailiffs in full regalia, and accompanied into town by over 1,000 gentlemen on horseback.

During the spring Assizes in 1724 the floor of the court collapsed. After years of discussion and planning the Shire Hall was rebuilt in 1770–72 replacing the medieval building with an elegant neoclassical building designed by London architect James Gandon, providing an austere backdrop to the 10 public hangings that took place on the steps outside. Between 1820 and 1840 two wings were added to the east and west side of Gandon's design. However, after a disastrous fire in December 1876 which destroyed all but the façade and grand jury room the Shire Hall had to be rebuilt again. This task went to Nottingham's best-known architect Thomas Chambers Hine. For this project Hine went for grandeur. The exterior of the Shire Hall dominates High Pavement, whilst the two courts with their oak-panelled walls are a prime example of Victorian extravagance. The courts remained in use until 1986 when the clocks were stopped at the time of the end of the last trial.

The County Gaol
The Victorian splendour of the courtroom is in stark contrast to the dark, squalid cells of the county gaol. The earliest gaol cells were probably on the ground floor of the medieval Shire Hall and in the caves below that. In around 1618 a new gaol was built at the rear of the old Shire Hall. The prison cells remain very much as they would have appeared to prison reformer John Howard when he visited the county gaol in the 1780s; dark and offensive dungeons and pits. However, efforts were made to improve the conditions; a new wing was built in 1833 to ease overcrowding, and gas lighting was introduced into all the cells in the mid 1850s. A chaplain and surgeon attended to the prisoners' spiritual and physical well-being, whilst efforts were made to teach prisoners to read and write. Later, following the lead from larger penal institutions, the 'separate system' was introduced, bringing order and discipline in the spirit of mid-Victorian reform. In 1853, the Chaplain reported to the Prison Inspector that:

the opportunities for misconduct have been greatly diminished of late by various improvements in the prison arrangements, viz., 'partial separation,' 'work,' 'school,' and 'evening reading.' The general conduct, especially of the convicts before they were separated and set to work, was troublesome ... but since the change even the worst seem reclaimed to peace and orderly behaviour and disposition.[1]

The majority of the long-term prisoners of the county gaol were debtors. The county gaol had separate living quarters for the debtors who had a greater degree of freedom. The remaining prisoners were those awaiting the outcome of their sentence – either transportation or execution – or petty criminals serving short stretches.

The County Police Station
High Pavement Police Station was headquarters for the Nottinghamshire County Police from 1847 to 1954. The present station was built in 1905 and housed the Chief Constable, Force Administration, CID and recruits. The Chief Constable's report of 1922 said they had only been able to build on a small piece of ground and they had 'always been very much cramped for room.' They had only been able to manage because the superintendent of the Nottingham Division was also the Deputy Chief Constable and lived in the Judge's lodgings. The present position, reported the Chief, was that the whole of the administration work of HQ was contained in five rooms, one of which was a telephone room, and the accommodation was only just adequate.

Work for the Nottingham Petty Sessional Division, which had a population of 130,000 circling the Nottingham area (the equivalent of a borough the size of Huddersfield) had to be done in two rooms. The superintendent living on the premises then had accommodation 'less adequate than any in England'. 'His wife not only has to act as police matron but also has to cook for the single men necessarily resident on the premises,' the Chief's report disclosed. 'This is a state of things which does not make for the maintenance of discipline ... No other County force in England with a similar strength is doing the work on anything like the same amount of ground,' he reported to Viscount Galway.[2]

In 1954 the County Force headquarters moved to larger premises at Epperstone Manor, and was officially opened by Sir David Maxwell-Fyfe,

Secretary of State for the Home Department. High Pavement police station then became a divisional headquarters and closed in 1985. However, the cells continued to be used as a court holding facility for a further two years. There was a separate cell for women prisoners, which contained a 'private' toilet and double bed.

The development of the Galleries
The idea to create a Museum of Law was the inspiration of solicitor Geoffrey Goldsmith, and was conceived in the 1980s. Geoffrey Goldsmith searched the entire country for the most appropriate site for the museum, before he finally settled on the Shire Hall in Nottingham. From this seed the Lace Market Heritage Trust, under the chairmanship of Mich Stevenson, established the Galleries of Justice in the early 1990s. After a successful fund-raising drive, with donations from Nottingham City Council, Nottinghamshire County Council, the University of Nottingham and Nottingham Trent University, Greater Nottingham TEC and the Royal Bank of Scotland among many others, the target of £3.5 million was reached, and the restoration and exhibition work began in 1994.

The Museum of Law Trust Company opened the Galleries of Justice to the public in April 1995. The museum incorporated the original 18th and 19th century county gaol and the Victorian civil and criminal court rooms in all their splendour. This was Phase 1 of the development of the museum. A year after opening the Galleries of Justice won the prestigious Gulbenkian Prize awarded for outstanding achievement. This was the first of many awards which were to follow.

In 1997 the museum began a £5.5 million development programme, Phase 2, as a result of significant funding from the Heritage Lottery Fund and European Regional Development Fund. In April 1998 Phase 2 of the development programme came to fruition with the opening of the Police Galleries housed in the Edwardian police station, built in 1905 adjacent to the Shire Hall. In July of the same year, the Galleries of Justice added the refurbished original bathhouse and laundry, medieval cave system, and a new transportation gallery to its Crime and Punishment exhibition and tour. 1999 saw the completion of the Phase 2 development with the opening of the Discovery Galleries on 2 April.

The new Gallery encompassed an exhibition on Civil Law, which was recently redeveloped into our community gallery, which is used to display artwork and projects that have been created by various community groups through project work undertaken with the museum and freelance artists; a temporary exhibition gallery, which enables us to curate short term exhibitions which focus on a wide variety of topics, including keepsakes made by convicts awaiting transportation, the Great Train Robbery, and the Krays; and a dedicated Children's Activity Centre.

In its short life, the Galleries of Justice has developed a national reputation, not only for its collections, but also for the atmospheric and interactive experience of three centuries of crime and punishment, along with its extensive educational and community work. In July 1997, the Galleries received the Heart of England Tourist Board 'Visitor Attraction of the Year' award after demonstrating high standards of customer service, excellent facilities and an innovative high standard of interpretation. 1998 will be remembered as a milestone for the museum, when it welcomed the Lord Chief Justice of England, Lord Bingham of Cornhill, as the inaugural President of the Galleries. The museum went on to receive the prestigious title 'Visitor Attraction of the Year (under 100,000 visitors)' in the 1999 England for Excellence awards. The judges considered it 'thought provoking and challenging, with proactive staff and themed throughout. Affordable for schools – we wish there were more educationally fun and entertaining ways to learn about our heritage like this.' In 2003 the Galleries of Justice was awarded the prestigious Gulbenkian Prize, the biggest arts award in the country, for its innovative and inspirational educational work through the Galleries National Centre for Citizenship and the Law (NCCL); and use of the museum's resources. Bamber Gascoigne, chair of the 2003 panel, commented:

> We were all immensely impressed by the dedication and inventiveness with which the whole staff of NCCL had tackled a very challenging problem – that of using their museum's rich resources to bring alive the potentially very dry subject of citizenship, whether in real-life cases re-enacted in authentic court rooms or through using the forbidding old prison to put crime and punishment in a historical perspective. Teachers will be grateful to them, and their experiment is one which others elsewhere will be able to follow and develop.[3]

The NCCL was a progression from the galleries of Justice's education and inclusion departments, which since 1995 have been running successful learning programmes for young people. It handles three main sectors: Schools and Colleges; Crime Reduction; and Community Access, all of which operate under the banner of citizenship, and aims to inform and challenge with an end result of citizenship learning. The Centre works with schools, colleges and the public to promote active citizenship in ways which are of real practical value to National Curriculum studies. The project also demonstrates the power of the arts in engaging participants in understanding, at first hand, the profound problems that relate to crime and punishment. Important community projects working with bodies such as the Home Office, the Probation Service and Nottinghamshire Police are just a few of the initiatives the Galleries' NCCL is involved in. As part of a series of projects, students are encouraged to think of new ways to interpret serious social issues, in order to develop their teamwork skills, build up their self-esteem and enhance their understanding of their community. Their work is expressed through video production and has produced some excellent results.

The Galleries of Justice is currently working toward the third phase of development. Following the HM Prison Service decision to close their museum in Rugby, the HMPS will transfer their entire collection to the Galleries of Justice. This will result in the refurbishment of the museum's 1833 prison wing to create a new and exciting exhibition space in order to display this nationally, if not internationally, important collection. Objects not displayed will be preserved in the Galleries' stores and made available to the public for research and viewing through the museum's Wolfson Study Centre. The museum is also planning to recreate a Victorian street, also within the 1833 prison wing, in order to increase the number of primary schools who come and use our educational facilities.

The collections
Through gifts, loans and the occasional purchase, the Galleries of Justice has acquired an extensive collection which is categorised into four main subject areas: police, prisons, legal and probation.

Police collections
The museum's police collection is dominated by the internationally recognised collections from Ross Simms and the Bramshill Police Staff College. These collections consist of over two hundred police uniforms and an extensive range of truncheons including one which was used during the Peterloo Massacre of 1819. The museum has actively collected a number of items of both regional and local importance to compliment these collections. Archive material related to the police ranges from standing orders, Superintendents' reports from the early 20th century, admission and discipline registers from the mid and late 19th century of Nottingham City Police, photographs of Nottingham City and Nottinghamshire Police dating from the mid 1800s to 1960s, and handbooks, as well as pocket books and personal documents from individual police constables. We also acquired the largest collection of restraints (A.R. Nichols Collection) in the United Kingdom, which date from the 1800s to present day.

Prison collections
As detailed above, the HMPS collection will form a new exhibition examining the history of prisons and the development of the Prison Service. In 2002 the museum acquired a number of scrapbooks containing letters written by Reggie Kray whilst in prison.

Legal collections
The Galleries' collection includes significant legal material. This has primarily been donated or on loan from legal families and private individuals. It is anticipated that the museum's legal collection will continue to grow and build on this already nationally important foundation. The collection includes material about individual legal personalities such as Lord Reading, and Lord Coleridge, as well as archival material and exhibits on both local and national cases, such as the Great Train Robbery, the A. A. Rouse case, and the local poisoning case of Nurse Waddingham as well as the handwritten autopsy notes of the leading pathologist Sir Bernard Spilsbury.

Probation & Reform Collection
The foundation of the modern Probation Service is often dated to 1876, when a journeyman printer named Frederick Rainer donated 5/- to the Church of

England Temperance Society (CETS) to arrest the inevitable downward spiral of those 'whose foot has once slipped'. The CETS responded admirably and appointed missionaries and mission women to the Police Courts who would befriend and assist those in need. By the end of the century every Police Court in London and Middlesex were so served, and in 1907 the first Probation Act was passed, formally creating the modern day Probation Service. The founding society continued until 1923, when the London Police Court Mission separated from the CETS. By 1961 it was clear that the terms 'Police Court' and 'Mission' were no longer appropriate and consequently the society changed its name to the Rainer Foundation. Fortunately the evolution of this foundation (and others associated with it, and assimilated by it) has been preserved, and the collection has come to be known as the Rainer Foundation archive. The collection includes report and minute books, photographs, pamphlets and records from 1820 to 1997. However, the development of the Probation Service is not the only facet of the archive. There is material on a variety of organisations and societies that contributed to the evolution of philanthropic endeavour, including the School of Discipline (established by Elizabeth Fry in 1825), the London Female Preventive and Reformatory Institution, various boys' homes, the Midnight Meeting Movement, and numerous Christian associations.

Conclusion

Nationally significant police, prison and legal material dominate the Galleries of Justice collections. Such material, together with the Shire Hall building complex, demonstrates the quality and uniqueness of our law collection.

Notes

1. Inspector of Prisons, *Annual Returns of Prisons Nottinghamshire, Nottingham County Gaol 1853*, p. 48.
2. Bill Withers *Nottinghamshire Constabulary: 150 years in Photographs* (Quoin Publishing: Huddersfield, 1989).
3. Speech at the Gulbenkian Awards Ceremony, Zandra Rhodes Fashion and Textiles Museum, London, 15 May 2003.

Galleries of Justice Collections Development Strategy, 2004

1. *Acquisition Policy*: The museum will seek to acquire artefacts relating to the Shire Hall and County Gaol, Nottingham.
   Development Strategy: To collect material which has been removed from the Shire Hall, including furniture and fittings such as court benches, clerk's chairs, sign boards, door fittings, keys, etc.
2. *Acquisition Policy*: The museum will seek to acquire artefacts relating to the police, prisons and courts of Nottingham and Nottinghamshire.
   Development Strategy: To collect material to interpret the Shire Hall prison, courts and police station. Concentrating on fixtures and fittings e.g. name boards, doors, locks, chains, furniture, regulations, procedural notices, etc. with local provenance.
3. *Acquisition Policy*: The museum will regard material relevant to the history of the police service in England and Wales as being an area for priority collecting.
   Development Strategy: To collect material that illustrates the development of the police in England and Wales, as well as its contemporary applications.
4. *Acquisition Policy*: The museum will seek to acquire prison collections of national importance, including those formerly held by HM Prison Service Museum.
   Development Strategy: To work with HM Prison Service to acquire the collections formerly of HM Prison Service Museum. To become the principal collector of artefacts relating to the Prison Service and to formalise this relationship with HM Prison Service in writing.
5. *Acquisition Policy*: The museum will seek to develop a comprehensive collection of artefacts relating to the judiciary and legal profession, including costume and relevant office equipment.
   Development Strategy: To collect a representative collection of costume relating to the different legal posts, including barrister, coroner, solicitor, different types of Judge (e.g. Circuit, High Court, etc.) and Lord Chancellor. This material is restricted to English and Welsh posts. The museum does not intend to collect historic European court costume but

does intend to collect contemporary costume now that European law has become more closely associated with UK law.

Also, to collect relevant office equipment. This will be restricted to type examples e.g. a partner's desk, clerk's stool, solicitor's chair, office presses (1 from each office), QC's lectern etc.

Also, the museum will seek to acquire relevant badges of office, including Law Society regalia, magistrates' badges, Bar Council regalia, Coroners Society medals (relating to personalities). Service medals will only be collected where they relate specifically to legal personalities.

6. *Acquisition Policy*: The museum will seek to display a representative or specimen collection of legal documents and seals. This may be achieved through collection or through loan.

   It is not the museum's intention to become a major collector of archive material. This is seen as the function of Record Offices. The intention is to seek a mutually beneficial relationship with such offices on a local and national basis. The museum will, however, form a representative collection of material. Where archives are collected for study purposes, the museum will abide by the guidelines set down by the Museum Association's Code of Ethics for Museums (2002) and RCHM's Standards for Record Repositories (1990).

   Development Strategy: To formalise the relationship between the Local Records Office, the Public Record Office and the museum.

   Also, to collect a representative collection of archive material including letters patent and other letters of appointment. This collection will be restricted to legal personalities or when the document or seal is of particular interest.

7. *Acquisition Policy*: The museum will seek to develop a specimen collection of illustrations, cartoons, etc. relating to all aspects of the law.

   Development Strategy: To collect court sketches where they relate to specific legal figures or cases. To collect a representative collection of cartoons relating to legal figures. To borrow a representative collect of prison art. To collect paintings inappropriate for other Registered Museums but relevant to the law.

8. *Acquisition Policy*: The museum will seek to develop a specimen collection of relevant printed ephemera.
   Development Strategy: To collect a relevant collection of court procedural forms, police procedural forms, prison procedural forms and bound record books (by type rather than location). To collect broadsides and newspaper cuttings directly related to specific cases and legal personalities.
9. *Acquisition Policy*: The museum will seek to develop collections relating to specific legal personalities.
   Development Strategy: To collect personal collections that represent the life and times of legal personalities. These personalities will be chosen from a broad range of legal posts, including Lord Chancellor, barrister, coroner, clerks, stipendiary and non-stipendiary magistrates and those legal figures whose judgments (rather than the cases involved in) have had a major impact on the English Legal System. For example, F E Smith, Lord Reading, Norman Birkett, Edward Marshall – Hall KC and Bernard Spilsbury are already represented in the collections. Collecting will be initially targeted to the following individuals:

   1. Bracton (13th century)
   2. Coke (16th)
   3. Hale (17th)
   4. Mansfield (18th)
   5. Blackstone (18th)
   6. Lord Denning★
   7. Sir Patrick Hastings KC★
   8. Lord Carson
   9. Lord Goddard★
   10. Lord Goodman
   11. Mr Justice Avory
   12. Lord Shawcross★

★collections already located.

10. *Acquisition Policy*: The museum will seek to develop collections relating to a representative range of court cases and to specific civil and criminal law issues.
    Development Strategy: To collect, where possible, a relevant range of cases which are of particular interest to demonstrate points of law.
    The museum will seek to collect evidential material, including exhibits in the following areas:

    (i) Contract Law
    a. Hadley v Baxendale (1854) 9 Ex 341
    b. Taylor v Caldwell (1863) 3 B & S 826
    c. Smith v Hughes (1871) LR 6 QB 597
    d. Foakes v Beer (1884) 9 App Cas 605
    e. Carlill v Carbolic Smoke Ball Co [1893] 1 QB 256
    f. Dunlop Pneumatic Tyre Co Ltd v Selfridge & Co Ltd [1915] AC 847
    g. Bell v Lever Bros [1932] AC 161
    h. Central London Property Trust Ltd v High Trees House Ltd [1947] 1 KB 130
    i. Scruttons Ltd v Midland Silicones Ltd [1962] AC 446
    j. McCutcheon v MacBrayne (David) Ltd [1964] 1 WLR 125

    (ii) Tort
    a. Rylands v Fletcher (1866) LR 1 Ex 265 ; (1868) LR 3 HL 330
    b. Hulton & Co v Jones [1910] AC 20
    c. Donaghue v Stevenson [1932] AC 562
    d. The Wagon Mound (No 1) [1961] AC 388
    e. Hedley Byrne & Co Ltd v Heller and Partners [1964] AC 465
    f. British Railways Board v Herrington [1972] AC 877
    g. Cassell & Co Ltd v Broome [1972] AC 1027
    h. Anns v London Borough of Merton [1978] AC 728
    i. Jones v Wright [1992] 1 AC 310
    j. Cambridge Water Co v Eastern Counties Leather [1994] 2 AC 264

(iii) Trusts
a. McPhail v Doulton [1971] AC 424
b. Barclays Bank Ltd v Quistclose Investments Ltd [1970] AC 567
c. Dingle v Turner [1972] AC 601
d. Gissing v Gissing [1971] AC 886
e. Commissioners of Income Tax v Pemsel [1891] AC 531
f. Boardman v Phipps [1967] 2 AC 46
g. Lipkin Gorman v Karpnale [1991] 2 AC 548
h. Re Astor's Settlement Trusts [1952] Ch 534
i. Chichester Diocesan Fund and Board of Finance v Simpson [1944] AC 341
j. Royal Brunei Airlines v Tan [1995] 2 AC 378

(iv) Constitutional/Administration
a. Beatty v Gillbanks (1882) 15 Cox CC 138b. Roberts v Hopwood [1925] AC 578
c. Ridge v Baldwin [1964] AC 40
d. Anisminic v Foreign Compensation Commission [1969] 2 AC 147
e. R v Barnsley Metropolitan Council ex p Hook [1976] 1 WLR 1052
f. Council of Civil Service Unions v Minister for the Civil Service [1985] AC 374
g. Att-Gen v Guardian Newspapers (No 2) [1990] 1 AC 109
h. R v Secretary of State for Transport ex p Factortame Ltd [1991] 1 AC 603
i. R v Secretary of State for the Home Dept ex p Brind [1991] 1 AC 696
j. M v Home Office [1994] 1 AC 377

(v) Criminal Law (* Artefacts located)
a. R v Dudley & Stevens (cannibalism case) (1884) 14 QBD 273
b. R v Bodkin-Adams (acquitted of poisoning patients) [1957] Crim LR
c. R v Armstrong (only solicitor to hang for murder) [1922] 2 KB 555
d. R v Craig and Bentley (murder of PC Miles) 1952 Times 10–13 December
e. *R v Mancini (acquitted for murder he later admitted to)

f. R v Camb (a 'no-body' case on an ocean liner) 1947 Notable British Trials
g. R v Christie (10 Rillington Place-Evans & Christie)
h. R v Biggs (Great Train Robbery)
i. R v Buck Ruxton (Doctor convicted of murder – forensic science evidence)

*Also: Krays and Richardson as examples of Gangland cases. The A6 murder Case (R v Hanratty) and Brides in the Bath case (R v smith (1915) 11 Cr App R 229

(vi) Land and Property
a. Midland Bank Trust Co v Green [1981] AC 513
b. Taylor Fashions v Liverpool Victoria Trustees [1981] QB 133
c. Williams & Glyn's Bank v Boland [1981] AC 487
d. Abbey National Building Society v Cann [1991] 1 AC 56
e. Street v Mountford [1985] AC 809
f. Federated Homes Ltd v Mill Lodge Properties Ltd [1980] 1 WLR 594
g. Bull v Bull [1955] 1 QB 234
h. Tulk v Moxhay (1848) 2 Ph 774
i. Walsh v Lonsdale (1882) 21 ChD 9
j. Wheeldon v Burrows (1879) 12 ChD 31

(vii) European Law
Type cases for European law have not yet been identified, as this is a new area of study.

(viii) Family Law and Industrial Tribunals
Cases to be sourced.

11. *Acquisition Policy*: The museum has a long-term aim to develop a representative collection of vehicles.
    Development Strategy: The Museum can currently care for and maintain three examples of transport. It is intended that they should represent major developments in their time e.g. An example of the first police motorbike or an early Black Maria.

12. *Acquisition Policy*: The museum will seek to develop representative collections reflecting technological advance in any aspect relating to the law, including for example, forensic investigation and computerised legal sources.
    Development Strategy: To collect material, which includes the following:

    > a. Early fingerprinting and the first case where fingerprinting was used – R v Jackson (burglary)
    > b. Photographic developments (e.g. image enhancing video as evidence, etc.).
    > c. Software (e.g. Holmes and DNA fingerprinting).
    > d. An early Lexis terminal

13. *Acquisition Policy*: The museum will seek to supplement its artefact collections with oral history recordings and copies of relevant archive film.
    Development Strategy: It is not the intention of the museum to create a film or oral history archive. Relevant copies may, from time to time, be acquired for educational or display purposes.
    It is the intention of the Museum, however, to create a database of their location within other public institutions. Examples may include:

    > a. Recorded interviews
    > b. Film, for example, of first police moped, the first time radios were used, etc.

14. *Acquisition Policy*: The museum will seek to collect items which relate to specific areas of cause and effect relating to changes or attitudes within and outside the law. These items are purely illustrative e.g. youth culture, cultural identity, campaign material, trade associations, pressure groups, law reform bodies, consumer groups etc.
    Development Strategy: To collect a representative sample of material from youth cultures, campaigns etc. This material will be restricted to English and Welsh items but will reflect multi-culturalism.

15. *Acquisition Policy*: The museum will seek to collect a representative number of items relating to material made in prisons.
    Development Strategy: To collect representative items made in prison and any items prior to 1877 when the National Prison Service was established.

Chapter Nine

Essex Police Museum

Martyn Lockwood

Over the years a number of attempts had been made to maintain a historical collection at police headquarters, but pressure on accommodation meant that it did not find a permanent home. Some of the collection was loaned to the Chelmsford and Essex Museum and much of the archival material was handed over to the care of the Essex Record Office. In 1989 the then Deputy Chief Constable, Peter Simpson, gathered together a group of both serving and retired police officers and other interested parties to look at the feasibility of establishing a police museum, to be based at police headquarters in Chelmsford.

The purpose of this paper is to look at the some of the issues that were faced by the Trustees of the museum in establishing a permanent collection and also ensuring the safety of the large amount of archival material which had been deposited with them. From the outset it was recognised that there was a need to ensure the permanency of the collection. To achieve this the first task undertaken was to establish the museum as a registered charity and this was achieved in 1994. The museum's mission statement was:

> The Museum was established to advance the education of the public

with regard to the evolution, development and role of policing in the County of Essex between 1836 and the present day.

A Board of Trustees[1] was formed which included, the son of a former Chief Constable of Essex (Sir Jonathan Peel).[2] A major step forward was achieved in 1998 with the appointment of a professionally qualified curator, who was employed for two days a week.[3] This has now been increased to two and a half days. Working within the Public Relations Department, their salary is paid by Essex Police. However there is no budget allocated to this role and any funding is by donations, research enquiries and sale of items in the museum.

In 1997 a Forward Development Plan was produced. The purpose of this was to identify those areas which needed further work and to produce a timetable to achieve them. The plan covered, among others, the following areas:

- Formal Tenancy Agreement
- Registration with the Museums and Galleries Commission
- Acquisition and Disposal Policy
- Documentation of Acquisitions
- Emergency Plan[4]
- Education Policy

The plan was included as a standing item on the agenda of all committee meetings in order that progress on the various issues could be monitored.

In 1999 the Trustees entered into a formal tenancy agreement with the Essex Police Authority for a period of ten years, handing over the lease of the museum to the Trustees. The rent for the ten years was one peppercorn! Full registration with the Museums and Galleries Commission was achieved in 2002.[5] This followed a lengthy period to achieve the requirements for recognition by the MGC. One of the major conditions was public access to the collection. Due to the location of the museum within police headquarters, visitors are only allowed access by prior appointment.[6]

In 2001 an Acquisition and Disposal Policy was drawn up. This document, to be reviewed every five years, set out clearly what items, whether by purchase, gift, bequest or exchange, could be collected by the museum. The policy also considered factors such as inadequate staffing, limited storage facilities and conservation resources when accepting an item into the collection. With regard to disposal, any item had in the first instance to be offered to a registered museum. In 2001 Essex Police produced a policy document covering 'disposal of assets'. This document defines the procedure to ensure that Essex Police achieves maximum benefit from the redeployment or disposal of surplus or redundant assets and scrap. This must be carried out in line with the Financial Regulation of the Police Authority. When considering the method of disposal consideration should be given at this point as to whether the item would be of interest to the Essex Police Museum (either for the museum to be given the opportunity to purchase or presented to the museum as a charitable donation).

Essex were fortunate in the matter of Records of Service (ROS). Registers naming every person who served as a police officer from 1840 have been kept and handed over to the care of the museum. (Two registers have been deposited at the Essex Record Office on long term loan.) In addition the records of service for all police officers since 1900 had been retained by personnel department.[7] Discussions were undertaken with them to ensure that they were not disposed of as 'surplus to requirement' and an agreement was drawn up to ensure they were handed over to the care of the museum when personnel had finished with them.

ROS would be retained by the personnel department for seven years after the individual to whom it related had left Essex Police. (This period of time is required to ensure that all potential outstanding personnel issues can be dealt with). At the end of the seven year period the personnel department review the ROS and, where appropriate, remove certain contents for confidential destruction. This will help ensure that the remaining contents are unlikely to cause substantial damage or distress to the individual. The Essex Police Museum would:

- ensure the secure preservation of those records and
- enable subsequent research using the ROS.

All the ROS passed to the museum remain the property of Essex Police Authority. The museum will undertake, through a written contract, to ensure that ROS are treated in accordance with Data Protection rules, other relevant legislation and force policy.

The general principle is that once a ROS has been passed to museum it will be closed for 100 years from the date of birth of the subject, or until their death, whichever is the sooner. This period is the 'closed period'. During the closed period, the subject, or a person nominated in writing by them, will have a right of access to the ROS free of charge and a right to obtain a copy of the ROS. Applications for access to ROS will be forwarded to the Secretary of the museum.

In 2000 the Trustees entered into a management agreement with the Police Authority. This was to be reviewed after five years. This agreement recognised that the collection was the property of the Police Authority and that items for the collection will be accepted on behalf of the Police Authority and must meet the conditions laid down in the Acquisition and Disposal Policy. Each year the Trustees submit an annual report for the information of the Police Authority. In 2004, in connection with the application for a grant from the Heritage Lottery Fund, this agreement was reviewed and renewed for a period of fifteen years. The basis of the agreement recognises that the preservation of the history of Essex Police is not a core function of the Police Authority and as a result it has handed over the day-to-day management and care of the collection to the Trustees of the museum. The agreement also requires a member of the Police Authority to be selected to sit on the Board of Trustees.

Education has always been considered a primary objective of the museum, especially in relation to young people. An Education Policy was written in January 2004, to formalise this. The mission statement contained with the policy states:

> The aim of the Essex Police Museum is to improve the public's knowledge and understanding of the changing role of the police in society since the early 19th century and to build bridges between the police and all groups in the community through the interpretation of its collection.

The policy considers matters such as target audiences,[8] marketing, displays and exhibitions, staff, volunteers, finance and funding.[9] The scope of the policy is based on a three year programme, after which it will be reviewed.

This article only offers a brief insight into the issues and problems that were faced by the Trustees and Committee in establishing the museum and ensuring its survival. We are quite happy to discuss any issues further and provide copies of the various policies if they can help others. Contact in the first instance should be made with
martyn.lockwood@essex.pnn.police.uk,
or sarah.ward@essex.pnn.police.uk

Notes
1. There are six trustees. The chairman is Peter Simpson, O.B.E.
2. Tony Peel – a distant relative of Sir Robert Peel. He was an Essex County Councillor, subsequently Chair of the Essex Police Authority and Chair of Essex County Council 2003/2004.
3. The museum did have the services of a Curatorial Advisor, employed by Essex County Council, who attended committee meetings and provided valuable advice.
4. This work has still not been undertaken.
5. Now the Museums, Libraries and Archives Council.
6. In 2003, some 2,500 visitors. Since April this year we have had over 1,000 visitors.
7. There are exceptions – including the ROS of the police officers killed during the Great War whilst on active service.
8. School groups based on the National Curriculum; children's groups and adult groups.
9. Including an application for a grant of £43,000 from the Heritage Lottery Fund to be used to re-display the museum and to appoint an education consultant to put together a National Curriculum based education programme.

Chapter Ten

Ripon Museum Trust: Filling the Gap

Ralph Lindley

Ripon Museum Trust was formed in 1981 as a direct result of influence from the Ripon Civic Society, which from its inception in 1968 had been concerned at the lack of museum coverage in the City of Ripon. The City Museum at Thorpe Prebend House had closed in 1956 and the small Wakeman's House Museum was under threat of closure. The Society had continued to press the local authorities to provide premises for another museum. In 1981 the old Ripon Liberty Prison which had been built in 1816 became vacant and it was decided to set up Ripon Museum Trust with the intention of opening the Ripon Prison & Police Museum in the premises. The aims of the Trust were, and remain: to provide and maintain a museum or museums in Ripon for the exhibition to the public of articles of historic interest; to extend, conserve, maintain and store the collections of the Trust, and to persuade the local authorities to provide museum facilities in the City to replace those lost by the closure of the Thorpe Prebend House and Wakeman's House Museums.

Membership is open to any person over the age of 18 years interested in furthering the aims of the Trust, and the Trust was granted charitable status in 1983. The Prison & Police Museum was opened in 1984 in the former prison in St. Marygate, which is owned by Harrogate Council. In 1994 the Trust obtained a lease from North Yorkshire County Council for the former Vagrants' Cell Block at the old Ripon Union Workhouse which was built in 1854 in Allhallowgate, and opened the Workhouse Museum there in 1996. At that time this was the first such museum in Great Britain. In 2000 the Trust opened up the old No. 1 Court in the court building, which was built in 1830 and which had closed in 1998, as the Courthouse Museum. The Prison & Police Museum and the Workhouse Museum are both registered under the Phase 2 Registration Scheme operated by Resource (now 'MLA', the Museums, Libraries and Archives council). The Courthouse has not been submitted for registration yet, due to the lack of a long-term lease from Ripon Cathedral which currently owns the building. It is anticipated that a long term lease will be granted within the next 12 months. The three museums are now known collectively as 'The Yorkshire Law & Order Museums'.

Ripon Liberty Prison was built as an extension to the House of Correction which was itself built in the seventeenth century. It closed in 1878 during a period when a wave of prison reform resulted in the closure of many small local prisons. In 1887 the City of Ripon lost its own police force when it was amalgamated into the West Riding Constabulary, and the old prison became the police station for that force in Ripon. It continued as the police station until the present one was built in 1956. We have managed to trace three police pensioners who actually served in the building and thus we now know the layout of the building when it was the police station.

The Trust is run by volunteers and survives on admissions and sales from the museums together with membership subscriptions. In 2002 we were awarded a grant from the Heritage Lottery Fund to renovate the Prison & Police Museum. This major work was only completed at the end of April 2004, and the museum re-opened on the 1 May. Since being awarded the grant we are now apparently seen to be 'successful' and have been awarded smaller grants from other organisations. This helps, but does not solve the problem of the lack of regular sources of funding which remains a constant concern. Many interesting items were found during the renovation work, including an old boiler dating from the middle of the nineteenth century which was discovered under the yard. This had to be removed and placed in a shelter in the yard at the Workhouse as it was right under the new reception area. Once it has been conserved it will be put on permanent display at the Workhouse as there is insufficient space for it at the Prison & Police Museum. It has already aroused interest amongst boiler enthusiasts as such boilers are somewhat rare. We have a large display about it in the Prison & Police Museum for the benefit of our visitors.

The Chief Constables of North Yorkshire Police, West Yorkshire Police, South Yorkshire Police and Humberside Police are all Patrons of the Trust. In the past, none of these forces have had an established museum of their own and the Prison & Police Museum is recognised as filling that gap. To date, North Yorkshire Police and West Yorkshire Police have handed their collections over to the Trust, and North Yorkshire Police have taken out corporate membership. The Trust has another Patron who is a recently retired Governor from H.M. Prison Service, which is about to close its own museum at their Training College at Newbold Revel, near Rugby. We have some artefacts from that museum on long term loan and are currently enlarging our own collection of prison items.

The three museums tell a unique story within the City of Ripon, since prisoners were incarcerated at the prison or police station and taken to the courthouse where a custodial sentence or transportation could be imposed, thus possibly depriving a family of their breadwinner with the inevitable result that the family ended up in the Workhouse in the days before the formation of the welfare state.

We have a very interesting case where two brothers who were infamous poachers were transported, one of them twice, to Australia. Elisha and John Sinkler, alias Hebden, of Pateley Bridge were notorious local poachers who often had violent encounters with local gamekeepers. Early in August 1831 the brothers severely beat up a gamekeeper named Barker employed by Mrs Lawrence of the Studley Estate on Dallowgill Moor. Arrest warrants were issued by Ripon Liberty Justices and on 18 of September the Ripon Liberty Head Police Officer, Samuel Winn, together with Thomas Dinsdale, the Ripon Sergeant-at-Mace and two Ripon Constables, Thomas Binns and Thomas Sweeting, went to Stonebeck near Pateley Bridge to arrest the brothers. They captured Elisha but his brother, John and a young man named William Longthorne effected a rescue. A violent struggle took place during which Thomas Dinsdale was stabbed. His wounds were quite serious although not fatal. New warrants were issued and notices offering ten guineas reward for each brother and Longthorne were posted throughout the area. On the 16 November 1832, Elisha was captured and he was delivered to York Castle to await trial at York Assizes. Shortly afterwards William Longthorne was also captured and delivered to York for trial. I strongly suspect that Elisha informed the police of Longthorne's whereabouts as there is certainly no honour among thieves – or poachers!

They were tried on 5 March 1833, were convicted of being accessories to wounding with intent to murder and sentenced to be hanged. This sentence was later commuted to transportation for 7 years. Elisha sailed for Australia on 30 May 1833 and arrived there on 18 October 1833. He spent his first months at the Convict Settlement at Port Arthur and was later hired out to work on a local farm. In 1841 he was granted a pardon and returned to England where he resumed his poaching. In 1843 he was involved in another stabbing incident and appeared before York Assize Court where on 4 March he was sentenced to transportation for life. He was sent to Australia for a second time but it is not known to which settlement he was allocated. He was again pardoned in 1856 and returned home. His brother, John had evaded capture for 10 years despite the posting of further reward notices until he was finally caught in March 1843. I suspect that for a second time Elisha turned informer and revealed John's whereabouts to the authorities, seeing no reason why he should suffer for a second time without his brother being brought to book as well. John was sentenced to death with an intimation that the sentence would be commuted to transportation, which was finally set at 15 years. He left for Australia on 13 March 1844. It is not known to which settlement he was allocated or exactly when he returned home. After their return home the brothers had enough money to purchase property in the area and continued their poaching. In 1871 they appeared before Ripon Liberty Court for poaching and threatening a gamekeeper. This time Elisha was fined £2 with costs and John was sentenced to 2 months hard labour in Ripon Liberty Prison which now houses the Prison & Police Museum.

In its archives, the Trust holds quite an assortment of interesting material relating to Yorkshire, although the majority of our holdings refer to the former North Riding Constabulary and other forces within that part of Yorkshire, as all the archive material once held by West Yorkshire Police has been passed to West

Yorkshire County Archives. We have a good cross section of archives which include such items as Police Warrant Cards, Police Station Inventories, Refused Charge Books, Visits to Licensed Premises Registers, Stray Dogs Registers, Accounts Books, General Orders, various publications for both World Wars, Civil Defence publications for Wartime and the Cold War period, Police Bail Books, Registers of Accidents, Charge Books, Conveyance of Prisoners to Gaol Books, Beat Information Books, Occurrence Books, Telephone Messages Books, Records of Visits to Prisoners in Cells Books, Registers of Offence Reports, and Annual Reports.

We are fortunate to have a potted history of police activity in the times of the North Riding Constabulary within the small market town of Bedale, thanks to the foresight of a police civilian employee who ensured that the books in question were not destroyed or sent to the rubbish tip. These cover the period from 1910 to 1965 and include Charge Books, Bail Books, Telephone Message Books, Refused Charges Books, Occurrence Books and Registers of Offence Reports. These have yet to be fully researched and we are looking forward to the information which will come to light as a result. Unfortunately a lot of the old personnel records of the former North Riding Constabulary were weeded – in other words shredded – some time ago and as a result a lot of interesting information was lost. The Trust is very lucky to have possession of the Appointments and Resignations Register which runs from 15 December 1896 to 31 March 1974. This covers the North Riding Constabulary (up to 1968) and the York & North East Yorkshire Police (1968 to 1974), but we have no idea if the first book with these details from the formation of the North Riding Constabulary in 1856 still survives and if it does where it is located. The register contains an officer's name and collar number, marital status, date of appointment, date of leaving Headquarters and station to which posted. These details are quite separate from the officer's name, number, rank, date of leaving, station vacated and cause of leaving (which could be Dismissed, Compelled to Resign, Resigned, Pensioned or during the time of war Joining His Regiment).

This was the case of my great uncle, Harry Crowther who joined the North Riding Constabulary on 3 February 1913 and was posted to Eston from where he left the force on the 31 May 1917 to join the Coldstream Guards. He returned to the force on 27 January 1919 when he went back to his posting at Eston. He retired in the rank of Inspector serving at Pickering on the 30 November 1941 and drew his pension until his death in February 1962. Much work has yet to be done to put all the information contained in this register on to computer so that names can be matched up from those in the appointments side with those in the resignations side.

We also have some details of appointments in the former Scarborough Borough Police. The Trust also has some Police Note Books from individual officers at various times throughout their service. We have an Inspector's Journal compiled by Inspector Benjamin Holmes of the North Riding Constabulary and who was stationed at Leyburn. This records his activities between 15 October 1905 and 28 June 1908. Amazingly, this book came to light after I had received a request from this officer's grandson for any information about his grandfather and his police service. He is shortly to have sight of the Journal together with other relevant information I have gleaned from the above mentioned Appointments and Resignations Register, old Police Almanacs, etc. A handwritten book of General Orders of the North Riding Constabulary begins with that issued by Thomas Hill, the first Chief Constable of the force, on 18 February 1857. The next entry is for four Defaulters – all Constables who were permitted to resign having been found drunk. This was quite a common occurrence at that time. The book goes as far as 1863 and gives a fascinating insight into life in the early days of that force.

In addition to the above items, we also have numerous smaller items which by themselves could appear to be somewhat insignificant, but when looked at in depth provide information which is not readily available in the usual archived items. By way of an example, in amongst a collection of Court Returns and other court papers from Bedale an envelope containing some of these documents was found to have the names and locations of North Riding Special Constables based at Catterick Police Station in October 1949. It is well known amongst police archivists that no permanent records were maintained in respect of members of the Special Constabulary by the relevant police forces.

Other examples of some of the other interesting items include an authorisation for Court Expenses at Whitby Court, and the fees account for the conviction of a pauper at Whitby Union Workhouse, both from 1886. We also have a notebook compiled by an unknown officer from the North Riding Constabulary, which contains photographs and details of local criminals from the first two decades of the 20th century. It was obviously made by him in a determined effort to be able to recognise any who dared to try and operate in his area. Material from the interwar period includes: the Police Gazette First World War Roll of Honour (Convicted Persons), dating from 1921; Christmas cards for the North Riding Constabulary in the 1920s and the West Riding Constabulary in the 1930s; and the North Riding Constabulary Motor Patrols Instruction Book from 1934. Material of interest from the Second World War includes the minutes of meetings of the Church Fenton Parish Invasion Committee, (1941 and 1942), and the North Riding Constabulary Fire Watching Rota for Northallerton (1942). Material covering the post-1945 period includes: warning notices for attendance at Assize and Quarter Sessions Court for P.C. John Redshaw of the West Riding Constabulary for numerous dates between 1943 and 1952; a telegram sent from Harrogate Police Station (in the West Riding Constabulary) to Easingwold Police Station (in the North Riding Constabulary) in 1948 regarding RAF Deserters; a document regarding the North Riding Constabulary's Wireless Communications (1948) and a number of lists of towns and villages in the East Riding Constabulary in 1953, the North Riding Constabulary in 1953 and York & North East Yorkshire Police in 1970. We also have West Riding Constabulary beat information cards, as carried by constables in the 1960s, which contained information relevant to their beat and section.

The Trust has acquired an additional room within the Prison & Police Museum as part of the renovation work and this is being dedicated as our Archive Room. Work has started to provide the necessary shelving and so on, and then the hard work will commence on the Archives themselves. Once established we shall offer research facilities to interested parties. The Archives are merely one part of our operation, as we have collections of various types of police and prison artefacts as well. While we specialise in Yorkshire-related law and order matters we also include general items and information to be able to present the general picture. The Trust was formed specifically to fill a gap in museums within Ripon and this we have achieved with a great deal of success. In the process we have ended by telling the law and order side of social history within Yorkshire in particular, purely by the way in which our buildings became available, and we believe that our operation is unique. We rely totally on our volunteers and are now looking at various ways of securing regular funding so we can continue to provide this service not only to the public of Yorkshire but also visitors who come to look at our wonderful county.

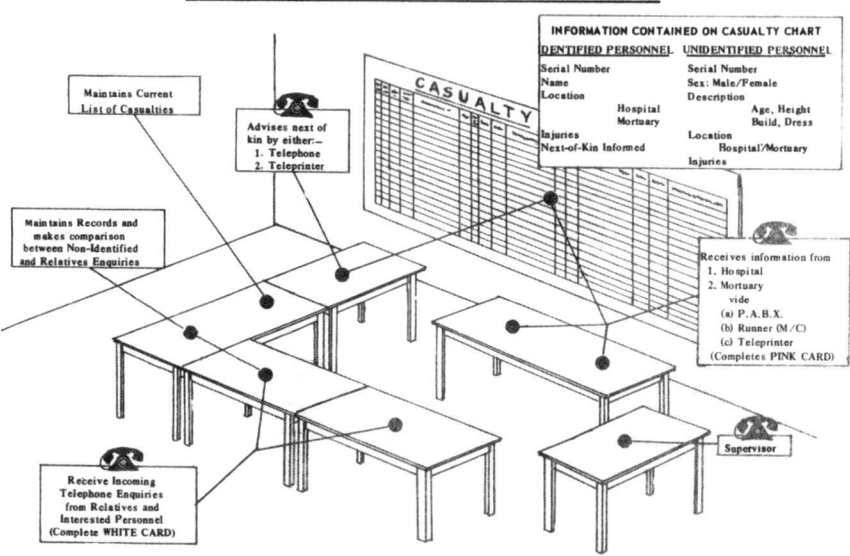

A page from the Surrey Police Major Incident Handbook, *1971. The nuts and bolts of police organisation can often be revealed in manuals such as this*

Part Four

Institutional Frameworks

Chapter Eleven

The Role of the Museum, Library and Archive Sector

Guy Purdey

This paper looks at the role of the MLA sector and how that relates to the history and heritage of the criminal justice system. It essentially breaks into three sections: the context, using the South East as an example of the issues that need to be considered by UK regions and home counties; the role of a museum, library and archive council and the MLA sector; links to, and benefits for, the heritage of the criminal justice system.

The South East is the largest region in England, covered by 19 County and Unitary Councils. It has the highest owner-occupation rate in the country and the lowest crime rate, but it also has the third highest number of unemployed people and significant areas of deprivation. Each of the English regions has a museum, library and archive council (MLAC). Their role is to act as the strategic development agency for the sector in their region, providing cohesion and developing synergies across museums, libraries and archives (the three 'domains' which make up the MLA 'sector'). They aim to enable museums, libraries and archives to fulfil their potential for public benefit, working on behalf of the national Museums, Libraries and Archives Council (MLA), the Government's principle advisor on the sector.

MLACs provide strategic leadership and advocacy, promoting and supporting areas such as access, learning and inclusion, and standards and stewardship. They provide information and advice on investment and funding, and support the sector by carrying out research and making shared data available. The South East is the largest English region with around 300 museums, 375 archives and over 2,500 libraries (including 498 public, 105 higher education, 102 health plus schools, workplace, government). Nationally, the figures are 2,500 museums, 2000 archives and 12,000 libraries receiving some 450 million visits a year. As well as working with their sector stakeholders, the MLACs work with their Regional Development Agencies, Regional Assemblies, Government Offices and other cultural agencies such as those for arts, sport and tourism for the benefit of the sector and the region. In the South East this has already led to shared posts and joint initiatives, such as one providing development and training for managers.

In terms of criminal justice heritage, the region has six museums specifically devoted to policing – Kent Constabulary; Newport Pagnell Police Museum; the Police Museum, Netley Training School, Hampshire; the Force Museums (Thames Valley Police); Surrey Police Museum and the Royal Military Police Museum in Chichester. This is only the tip of the iceberg, however, in terms of the broader history and heritage of criminal justice. Many other institutions hold and interpret material relevant to this wider heritage. Examples include Rochester Guildhall Museum, with its displays on prison hulks and links to the Admiralty Court; Margate Local History Museum housed in a building complete with courtroom and cells and Horsham Museum, with its links to prison reform and material relating to John George Haigh, the acid bath murderer (tried in the town), to name just a few. Libraries like the Bodleian in Oxford have wide-ranging collections including material relevant to this theme, as of course do archives, from records of county Assizes and lists of transportees to archive material linked to policing.

One of SEMLAC's jobs as a regional agency is to promote the attainment and maintenance of standards. These vary from the specific, such as Museum Registration, to more generic legal requirements such as those relating to the

Disability Discrimination and Freedom of Information Acts. Registration is a minimum standards scheme which helps to assure interested parties (such as potential object donors and funding bodies) that a museum is well run, likely to continue operating over the longer term and, in principle, worthy of funding support. SEMLAC administers the Scheme in the South East, and there are currently 267 museums registered (about 1,850 nationally). To help museums meet the requirements of the DDA, SEMLAC has supported programmes of access audits co-ordinated at County level to identify what they need to do and put in place realistic plans to achieve it. Linked training has helped to address misconceptions and dispel sometimes unfounded concerns.

'Stewardship' is a slightly obscure term, defined by MLA in its *Benchmarks in Collection Care* (Resource, London, 2002) as: 'The whole range of demands and responsibility associated with the management of cultural heritage collections.' Across museums, libraries and archives other related terms used include 'collection management'; 'preservation' and 'collections care', all of which have overlapping definitions. Like the UK and US we are sometimes divided by a common language! For SEMLAC what it means is 'the bigger picture', rather than just conservation or restoration. This includes records of ownership; storage and physical protection; environmental monitoring and control; security; cataloguing and access; handling procedures; cleaning; exhibition and loan procedures; emergency planning; use of surrogates (copies, replicas etc) and digitisation. It is our job to get a handle on the bigger picture across the region. As a new agency, two years ago we started with very limited baseline information of what the region has and what it needs across the whole MLA sector. Nevertheless, bringing together museums, libraries, and archives presented certain obvious benefits. Archives, for example, bring with them a significant number of conservation labs and expertise in the treatment of paper and similar materials. SEMLAC's role is to pull all this together, promoting networks, making links, spotting the gaps, targeting existing resources where they can do the most good and making the case for new ones.

To meet this challenge, we launched a series of research projects to improve our picture of the region, along the way identifying case studies of where institutions were doing things well to share with others and helping some individual institutions work out their own specific needs. One of these projects was the

'Collections Care and Management Provision and Needs Survey'. This has produced a mass of useful information which has helped to inform our work, for example on the subject of emergency planning. Only 54% of respondents to the survey had an emergency plan, and less than that actually maintained equipment to support it or had rehearsals and reviews. Coupled with the fact that emergency planning will be part of the revised Museum Registration Standard, this identified a clear regional need. SEMLAC commissioned and is running training to meet it. 68% of respondents also thought that co-operative response networks at a more localised, 'sub-regional', level for mutual assistance in the event of an emergency would be useful, and SEMLAC will be looking to facilitate their creation.

So what the links to, and benefits for, the heritage of the criminal justice system? How can this help us care for and share our history and heritage? This can happen in a number of ways, drawing on the resources, knowledge and support of the wider museums, libraries and archives community. Just a few of the possibilities are described below.

Subject/Theme networks
There are moves to establish these across museums, libraries and archives for mutual support, co-ordination and collaboration. An example is the Rural Museums Network (RMN), centred on the Museum of English Rural Life at the University of Reading (http://www.ruralmuseumsnetwork.org.uk/) The network has a website and email discussion group and has been working on a database project to help identify the 'distributed National collection' for its theme. This will help pinpoint not just who has what and where, but will also provide a resource to assist object identification and a way of seeing if key types of material are under-represented, falling into the danger of being lost without trace or record. Similarly, waste of resources on unnecessary duplication can be avoided by sensible co-operation. A similar example is the Maritime Collections Strategy (http://www.ukmcs.org.uk/) agreed across the country by maritime museums to clarify exactly who is responsible for collecting under certain themes (e.g. the history of the fishing industry). Groups like these could develop joint projects, for example to tackle cataloguing, sharing knowledge or people to get the job done.

SEMLAC is looking to support and facilitate such groups. Would 'Criminal Justice History and Heritage' make a good co-operative network? Of course, there are already well-established groups looking at aspects of this theme, a principal one being the Police Historical Society (PHS). Any new group would have to offer something more, or different, to be worthwhile. Looking at how the RMN functions, one element is its email discussion list. At present, people working with criminal justice materials can post a query on the PHS website and be put in touch with a wide range of people with great expertise to get an answer. An e-list could build on this and other deep wells of knowledge, to offer a wider and more creative experience, with the opportunity for debate, discussion, and the sharing and development of ideas and good practice. Such lists can help address the problems faced by people working in isolation with this kind of material – RMN includes members with major relevant holdings but for whom agricultural heritage is not the only theme.

A broader network like this could tackle other aspects of criminal justice history (e.g. prison reform), and could help to re-forge links between artefact collections and related records held in other institutions (see below). Easily set up, such an e-list is, however, only as good as the people on it and their willingness to contribute. Nevertheless, it might be a good first step towards the development of a more concrete network, while being useful in itself, even if it goes no further than that.

Shared issues and support
Everyone who attended the conference shares a subject area in common. In addition, though, we also share many themes and issues with the holders of other types of collection. This offers scope for support through wider networks. For example, uniforms are a big issue for military museums and, indeed, any museum with costume/textile collections will share similar concerns: such issues can be tackled together. In the 1990s, Surrey Museums Consultative Committee (a co-operative network of all the local authorities and museums in the county) carried out a project to examine and address the needs of textile collections in museums in its area. MLACs can provide access to training and support. In addition to working with the National Preservation Office and Blue Shield (the cultural equivalent of the Red Cross) to provide emergency plan-

ning training, SEMLAC is also making available help with forward planning through the organisation 'Arts and Business'.

Groups with needs in common can develop projects which have a better chance of securing funding because of their shared benefits. The 'Private Faces in Public Places' project, funded by the Heritage Lottery Fund through the Access to Archives Scheme, allowed a number of institutions to share the services of two archivists to tackle cataloguing needs and train non-specialist staff. The developing network of museum Hubs across the country is another emerging resource from which others will be able to benefit. In the South East a key issue for the Hub is collections care, and it is establishing a skills bank to allow it to share its knowledge.

Legal issues in common
MLA sector organisations are facing up to their responsibilities under a number of relatively new legal requirements, including Freedom of Information, Data Protection and the Disability Discrimination Act. As well as the general advice available, bodies like MLA and the National Archives have more specific help on offer. Those worrying about FOI could visit http://www.pro.gov.uk/about/foi.htm where the National Archives explores its approach and supplies some useful model documents. On the DDA, the MLA website at http://www.mla.gov.uk/action/learnacc/00access_03.asp has downloadable copies of its Disability Portfolio (Resource, London, 2003) which offers excellent guidance and links in access good practice and meeting your responsibilities under the Act.

Collections and communities
In a forthcoming project, SEMLAC will be looking at collecting policies in institutions across the region and good practice in making collections genuinely integrated with, and relevant to, communities. For police museums in particular, there are many parallels with regimental collections and the need to interpret the wider social history side of the picture, through, for example, oral history records with the families of servicemen, and the communities around barracks. Military museums play multiple roles which can include public relations, recruitment and maintaining *esprit de corps* and here too, police museums

might find something of value, a point echoed in other papers in this volume.

Working with communities can, in addition, offer wider interpretive viewpoints and can help to tackle intrinsic imbalances in the records. For example, the 'legalistic'/place of deposit origins of many record office collections leads to much 19th century material being dominated by minute books. This, in turn, leads to a near invisibility of women in the picture presented, one that could be addressed by a more rounded approach to collecting, looking at diaries and personal correspondence. The social history materials of local museums could also complement and provide context to the interpretation of police collections, as could local studies libraries and archive records, helping to balance an 'organisation-focused interpretive voice' – one which sees everything from the point of view of the police force in question. Some relevant collections are already held and interpreted in other museums, providing potential examples of a broader context of interpretation and again, the papers presented here have something to offer on this.

Some examples and the question of funding

For those seeking other examples, a visit to the 24 Hour Museum website at www.24hourmuseum.org.uk is well worthwhile. The following brief selection of case studies from it highlight a number of the points made above. Continuing the theme of collections and communities, the case of the Mobile Police Museum, teaching Yorkshire schoolchildren about the history of policing, is an example of police/public relations at work (although it is, in fact, run by an independent enthusiast). In addition, this initiative was funded by a grant from the Coalfields Regeneration Trust, and demonstrates the importance of lateral thinking in seeking out funding sources. Grant-giving bodies have a range of criteria and themes which they want to support, from education to crime prevention. What can you do that brings your aims and theirs together? SEMLAC has been working to develop a database of funding sources, broken down by theme. In addition, your regional Heritage Lottery Fund team hold regional surgeries so that you can explore your ideas face-to-face.

Working with other institutions to put criminal justice themes into a broader context is well illustrated by the London Canal Museum's initiative to re-capture the history of the canal constabularies. In partnership with the British

Transport Police archivist, the museum put out an appeal for information and material to support a special exhibition. A totally different example of the police and local museums in co-operation comes from a museum's comic book project in Manchester. Distributed widely in the community, these tell 'real-life stories about how people from Manchester's Black and Asian communities have engaged with exhibitions and collections in the region.' The aim is to promote social inclusion and overcome assumptions that culture is for the white middle classes, and one story shows how police and local children came together in a museum in Bolton.

Articles on each of these projects currently feature on the 24 Hour Museum website, the first two by David Prudames and the last by Heidi Dore.

What objects mean

Objects mean far less without the supporting records that explain what they are and give them a place in relation to people and events. Again there are parallels in the wider MLA sector with challenges facing some aspects of criminal justice heritage. As an example, the museums of some mental health hospitals hold objects relating to the history of the institution and its patients but the archive record is held elsewhere, sometimes in a local archive office, as the result of effective records management systems within the institutions during their operation. This has been highly successful in ensuring the survival and proper care for these records, and leaves scope to re-forge links with the object collections which have been preserved by a different mechanism, which might otherwise not have been possible, achieving a fuller picture and benefits for all parties and their users.

That leads to a last key point – it is not just about objects, it's about people. Museums, libraries and archives have a role to play in citizenship and in promoting social inclusion. A few years ago the PAT10 report from Government highlighted the role of culture in combating social exclusion and promoting wider understanding. One of the examples quoted was the Galleries of Justice in Nottingham and its successful work with young people at risk of offending (and another successful initiative in this area happened at the Angel Row Gallery in the city). In the South East, museums like Amberley in West Sussex have a track record of projects with prisoners and ex-offenders, developing skills and contributing to resettlement. This is part of the history and heritage of the criminal justice system itself and also offers the potential for other museums, libraries and archives to learn about the system from those in the field, providing another opportunity to share their skills in return.

The Black Box Project, co-ordinated by SEMLAC, established links with prison inmates, ex-offenders and vulnerable individuals (e.g. street sleepers). Through a creative scheme involving museums in West Sussex and Brighton, it aimed to give a voice to those seldom heard and demonstrate that museums have a role to play in the lives of everyone, including 'non-traditional' users. As part of Black Box, participants were invited to take part in a series of workshops led by poets and supported by museum staff and artists. Inspired by artefacts brought in by museums, and working only with images and words, participants created their own 'personal museums'. Usually, as one participant in the project put it: 'There are no people like us in museums.'

As well as its impact on those who took part, the project had a number of wider outcomes, including guidance on how to do this kind of work. Since then, SEMLAC has led new initiatives such as 'Project Hero', working with young offenders, again leading to wider training and guidance and is now working on a cultural diversity tool kit. Black Box is a good place to end, because it draws together the past and the present of the criminal justice system: In Horsham the town's museum was one of those where prisoners' work from the Black Box Project (inspired by its artefacts) was exhibited. Horsham was also the location of arguably the world's first reforming gaol, and, in a pleasing piece of historical continuity, Black Box brings its links with prison reform right up to date.

Chapter Twelve

The Effect of Freedom of Information on Records and Archives Management

Kelvin Smith

It almost goes without saying that there are many, many competing priorities in most walks of life, not least in public authorities. This is one of the reasons why managers and other personnel in that sector have yet to get fully to grips with an important piece of legislation that was passed in November 2000 – the Freedom of Information Act. Three and a half years have passed very quickly and the date when the provisions of the Act have to be brought fully into operation (1 January 2005) is almost upon us. The public are probably even more unaware of the legislation, but this situation is about to change dramatically. Soon there will be publicity and very many people, from many professions and occupations, will be anxious to take up the new opportunities.

This article assumes that the reader is aware of the major provisions of the FOI Act:

- right of access to recorded information held by public authorities irrespective of its date
- unless an exemption applies and there is no overriding public interest in disclosure

- 20 working days to confirm or deny that information is held and provide it
- duty to provide advice and assistance
- enforcement by the Information Commissioner
- publication schemes
- fees
- appeal procedures
- codes of practice

What does the Act mean for the public? Freedom of Information is part of the government's constitutional reform agenda, and is particularly about transparency and accountability in the public sector. It means an opportunity to find out what publicly-funded bodies do and how they do it. The public will seek information not only about policies in general but also about things that impinge on their own lives. It is aimed primarily at current information but applies also to archives.

What does it mean for records managers and archivists? Section 46 of the Freedom of Information Act provides authority for a Code of Practice on the Management of Records. This high level document is compulsory reading for all records managers and their staff. The rationale behind the Code is simple – if the quality of records and archives management is not good, public authorities have no chance of meeting the requirements of the FOI Act. Records management matters for FOI. The legislation cannot be implemented if public authorities do not know what information they hold and where it is, and cannot retrieve it when requested to do so. Records management policies and procedures overcome these problems.

The National Archives has developed model action plans for achieving records management compliant with the Code of Practice – recommended by the government Advisory Group on Openness in 1999. There are six such models available for:

- Central Government
- Local Government
- Further Education and Higher Education Organisations
- Police Authorities

- National Health Service
- Schools

The models are available through the National Archives website (www.nationalarchives.gov.uk/foi/)

The plans identify nine major steps in reaching records management compliance:

1. Establish the Records Management function
2. Have a records manager in place and confirm the function's roles and responsibilities
3. Issue a records management policy statement
4. Develop training and awareness programmes for all staff
5, 6 & 7. Ensure that important activities of the records life cycle are in place, including:
   - adequate storage
   - documentation of appraisal and disposal
   - good tracking systems
8. Document disclosure and exemption decisions in order to:
   - handle appeals
   - promote consistency in dealing with requests
9. Measure the performance of the records management system

The nine steps for effective records management set out in the model action plan above are put into practice through the following actions:

The records management function
Coordinate approach to the management of information. Ensure that records management is recognised as a specific corporate function within a public authority and that it has the necessary levels of organisational support (not just an add-on to another unit). Good records management is a benefit, not a burden. It is not just for implementing FOI – it is an integral part of business efficiency, ensuring that information is easily accessible, that processes and procedures are properly documented, and that decision-making and actions are undertaken with confidence.

Roles and responsibilities of records and archives managers

Every public authority should have one or more people who are responsible for the management of its records from the moment they are created to the time of their disposal. Their roles and responsibilities should be known throughout the organisation. The Records Manager should be a key member of staff, with a level of authority that will enable them to get things done. They should have the appropriate qualifications and/or experience to carry out the requirements of the Code of Practice effectively.

Records management policy statement

Manage business information effectively by providing an authoritative statement on the management of records. The policy statement should have the same weight as other major policy issues (for example, health and safety, equal opportunities). It should include:

- mandate for all records management functions
- commitment to create, keep and manage records
- role of records management
- relationship to overall strategy

It should be short and to the point so that it will be easily read and understood by all staff in the organisation. It must serve as a framework for supporting standards, procedures and guidelines.

Training and awareness

Ensure that records staff are appropriately qualified, trained or experienced, and that all staff understand the need for records management. Good record keeping becomes the responsibility of everyone under FOI. Awareness may take several forms – a records management element in induction programmes, use of the intranet, departmental forums, newsletters and formal meetings. Formal training is available from several sources – universities (records and information management courses are offered by Liverpool, Northumbria, Wales/Aberystwyth and University College London), professional associations and societies, the National Archives, and private organisations.

Records creation and management
Keep information in a well-structured records management system so that it can be identified and retrieved when required. A corporate filing system (paper and/or electronic) should form the basis of an organisation's information resource. A standardised referencing system ensures a clear record exists of how various series of records were created, by whom they were created, when they were created and for what purpose – important in meeting the demands of freedom of information legislation and in providing contextual information for business managers and future researchers; it promotes the systematic and economical storage of records in all formats, and the timely retrieval and tracking of records (crucial in a freedom of information regime); it enables the ready identification of records for answering enquiries or for appraisal, and prevents the duplication of information between units/sections, which can have serious consequences if the organisation is unsure which holds the authentic and reliable information. Record classification schemes should be based on function not by organisation, team or type of record. In this way records will be less susceptible to disruption when the organisation's structure changes

Record maintenance
Maintain authentic records over time by providing appropriate protection of records throughout their life cycle. Ensure that storage and handling of records, even when they are not in current use, is adequate. Whereas, in the past, closed records which had to be kept for a set number of years (often to satisfy either legislative requirements or business needs) were packed, stored in basements and forgotten about until their disposal date, such records may now be the subject of FOI requests. They should, therefore, be stored and handled with that possibility in mind. All organisations should have business recovery plans – procedures to adopt in the event of a disaster. They should identify what are their vital records – those records without which they could not carry on the business should a disaster occur.

Record disposal
Ensure that information is disposed of in accordance with agreed procedures and that selection and disposal decisions can be explained by careful documen-

tation of the appraisal and disposal of records. Almost the only reason for keeping records is to run the business of the organisation. When that reason ceases to apply, the records should be destroyed. There may be a necessity to keep some records for legal reasons (financial information, property deeds, etc) or for historical value, but these are greatly outweighed by the business need. Disposal schedules are a key element of an organisation's records management policy. They are timetables that set out when series or groups of records are due for disposal, whether by destruction or transfer to an archive. They make it easy (for both staff and public) to identify whether information exists. Disposal schedules should always be available in publication schemes.

Monitoring implementation
Document disclosure and exemption decisions so that they are consistent, and can be explained and referred to in the event of appeals or reports to the Information Commissioner. A system to track FOI access requests will help to ensure that the organisation meets the statutory deadlines and deals with requests consistently (for example, that different parts of the organisation or sector are applying exemption criteria in the same way to the same types of information).

Performance measurement
Identify whether information is being managed effectively through monitoring of compliance with records management policies and procedures. Guidance on performance indicators is available from a number of sources, such as professional associations and the British Standards Institute.

Information technology links
Another crucial aspect of the implementation of freedom of information is its link with other developments in information management – not least the strategy for e-government. The electronic delivery of services to business and the citizen will depend on good management of electronic records. Up to now new information systems do not always generate electronic records that fall under any formal corporate control and management. Meeting government targets on modernisation means that records managers and others have to look carefully

at the processes of managing information in this (and other) formats. They must:
- know what records are out there in the organisation
- develop a policy for the effective management of the records
- evaluate the records for retention
- prepare sustainability strategies for maintaining access to, and reliability of, electronic documents identified as having continuing value

Many of the processes under freedom of information are similar to, if not the same as, those required for effective electronic records management. Records managers, therefore, must be working closely with IT colleagues. We do want to risk duplication of effort or re-inventing the wheel.

The two initiatives of FOI and e-government have led to a great increase in the formal guidance on records management that the National Archives makes available. This is principally aimed at central government departments and agencies but can be adapted and used by anyone. The guidance comprises a set of standards, currently undergoing revision, on major aspects of the management of paper records (such as file creation, tracking records and disposal scheduling), retention scheduling guidelines for those records that most, if not all, organisations create and manage – records relating to buildings, accounting, personnel, health and safety, internal audit, etc. – and publications on particular records management issues, such as human resources (which includes a competency framework for records management staffing), information surveys, access to public records, and a guide to the Data Protection Act 1998.

Finally, I mentioned at the beginning of this piece how important freedom of information legislation is for both public and public authorities. This quote from the Code of Practice on the Management of Records, says it all:

> Any freedom of information legislation is only as good as the quality of the records to which it provides access ... Consequently, all public authorities are encouraged to pay heed to the guidance in the Code.

Records and information management procedures need to be of a very high standard in the modern world of increased accountability, expectations of the public, and greater business efficiency. Records and information managers are not only crucial to ensuring that freedom of information procedures are implemented effectively but also to ensuring that our heritage is safely protected and made available for those who want to study it.

Chapter Thirteen

Police Force Records Management Policies and the Needs of the Historical Record

Alice Stewart

Records management may not be a new profession, but it is a relatively unusual in police forces. Strathclyde Police was the first force in Scotland and possibly the UK[1] to appoint a professional records manager/archivist. In four years following, the situation has changed radically. Six of the eight Scottish forces now employ records manager/archivists. The Scottish Drug Enforcement Agency has recently advertised a similar post. This is a positive development for records management and archives alike. There are those that believe that records management has the potential to damage the preservation of historical records. This does not have to be the case; rather than being detrimental, records management can have a positive impact on historical records.

The needs of the historical record

What are the needs of the historical record? A long and detailed list of requirements can easily be gathered, but they can be grouped under three general headings: intellectual preservation, intellectual control and physical preservation. A record, its information content and context must first be recognised as having ongoing value and be retained as evidence of a transaction, activity or function. Thereafter, search tools, controls over access, authenticity, provenance, security and confidentiality are essential to manage the record. Finally, the record, whether on paper, microfilm, computer, audiotape, vellum or parchment, must be stored preserved and conserved in the best way to ensure that it is physically available in the future.

But do the needs of historical records differ from those of records? These criteria can just as easily be applied to operational and administrative records in a police force or indeed any organisation used in the day-to-day operation of its business. The needs of all records are the same, however the practical steps implemented to meet these needs may vary.

Compare a nineteenth-century station occurrence book with a invoice received last week. Appraisal of these records attributes a value; the occurrence book is of historical value, while there is a legal requirement to retain the invoice for six years. The occurrence book must be described and catalogued, placed in context within the police collection, indexed and measures must be taken to secure its provenance, security and use. The invoice must also be indexed and accessible, placed in context among the other 70,000 invoices the Force receives each year, while keeping it secure from misuse and tampering. Finally, measures must be taken to ensure that the occurrence book is stored in an acid free box, in conditions of optimum humidity and temperature and that it is not accessed or exhibited in conditions that will physically damage it. This is the best way to ensure that the document that has an archive value will still be available for future generations to enjoy. However, the invoice has a much shorter life and therefore conditions do not have to be so ideal or expensive. It must be protected from water and fire, but temperature and humidity do not have the same relevance and it may be considered an acceptable risk to use the invoice while enjoying an 11 o'clock coffee, which is entirely unacceptable with a nineteenth-century occurrence book.

Practice before records management
The historical records of Strathclyde Police and its 40 or so former forces and constabularies are deposited in Glasgow City Council Archives where they are

preserved and managed on behalf of the Force. Most Scottish forces have a similar agreement. It is an excellent arrangement for the records and the two organisations. The Strathclyde collection dates from the establishment of the City of Glasgow Police in 1800 and comes up to date to 2004 with records from the current Strathclyde Force. As well as administrative records, the collection includes personnel records of police officers from the 1820s to 1985. As might be expected the survival of records is patchy; there are unexplained gaps in the personnel records that frustrate family historians, while detailed records of cases investigated are few and far between. Why should that be the case? The records belonged to many separate forces that gradually amalgamated, records were lost or mislaid during office moves, no one knew they were valuable or thought that they were worth keeping and because no one took responsibility or offered guidance and direction to ensure their survival. In other words, their intellectual, administrative and physical needs were not always managed. The collection survived by good fortune and was finally deposited in Strathclyde Regional Archives at the local government reorganisation in 1975 when the present Strathclyde Force was formed. There was no deposit agreement that either Archives or the Force can find. This situation is not unusual and is mirrored elsewhere in Scotland. Records were also retained by force museums. A large and significant collection was recently deposited in the Archives from the Strathclyde Force Museum. These records were not publicly accessible, available or properly preserved.

In short the needs of historical records were not being met in a structured way prior to the introduction of records management. Their survival depended to a great extent on luck and having an officer with an interest in history to realise that they should not be destroyed when space was needed for new filing. Records management is not diverting resources from historical records because resources were not generally allocated to them before.

Nature of historical records
Records are changing. Registers and ledgers, duty and occurrence books, and books of photographs of criminals belong to the past. If historians wait for this type of information to filter through on new formats, trusting fate to ensure survival, they will be disappointed. Nor can decisions on selection, control and

preservation wait until records have fulfilled their initial administrative usefulness. In common with all other forces, Strathclyde Police logs, records, investigates, manages and reports crimes and incidents electronically. While notebooks[2] are still in use, for some crimes it is entirely conceivable that they will be the only manual records associated with that case. Over half the records in Strathclyde are born, live and die electronically. Station occurrence books once used to log crimes and events have been replaced by computer generated statistics based on postcodes. Electronic records and modern paper in particular need specific rules and standards for intellectual control and physical preservation. Fate cannot be trusted to ensure the survival of records because modern recording formats do not have the permanence of past methods.

Records management policies
What is meant by records management policies? A wide range of policies has been developed to improve administrative practice and support operational needs. They also address legislative and regulatory requirements, for example the s61 Code of Practice on Records Management under the Freedom of Information (Scotland) Act 2002 requires public authorities for the first time to retain lists of records destroyed. In addition they form the basis for compliance with e-government initiatives that are underway, assist in the join-up of service provision while ensuring security, authenticity and accuracy.

In Scotland the Association of Chief Police Officers Scotland (ACPOS) has a new records management sub-group and has developed a number of standard policies and guidance documents. The first of these is the ACPOS Model Action Plan[3] prepared to assist Forces in the early stages of FOI implementation. It is very heavily modelled on the Lord Chancellor's original and the generic Scottish version, but has been updated in police-friendly language and was aimed at police officers rather than specialists in the field. It has proved a useful tool in demonstrating the amount and nature of work that has to be carried out and has been a significant factor in having specialist archivist/records managers appointed. Section 8 in the ACPOS MAP makes reference to the development of retention schedules and the need to retain archives to document the history of the force is included.

> A detailed records retention and management schedule must be compiled. This document lists types of records and how long they are kept for. Compilation must take into account the legislative, statutory, regulatory, business and operational needs of the force as well as identifying those records that should be retained permanently to document the history of the force...

Stage 12 of the same document is specifically aimed at archives and historical records. The accompanying text reads:

> Forces are unlikely to have the appropriate skills and resources to manage their historical archives and therefore it is recommended that arrangements be made to regularly transfer records to a local archive office where they can be made accessible. These records are held on behalf of the transferring authority (unless the terms and conditions of transfer stipulate a transfer of ownership). Records transferred must be included in the force publication scheme. Under s.25 of the Act and part 3 of the Code those records would then be taken to be reasonably obtainable and so would constitute exempt information for the purposes of the Act. This means that forces are not required to provide the information in response to a request under the Act, instead can explain that the information is available from the public archive and provide contact details.
>
> To allow the public archive to administer these records, the transferring force must review records prior to transfer and provide details of records that should not be made public, citing relevant exemptions, why and for how long they apply.

The ACPOS MAP is not mandatory but it has already been successful and if followed will achieve its aims. Perhaps most significant is that for the first time historically valuable records are included in a high level strategic document.

ACPOS has also developed a schedule of recommended retention periods that Forces have subsequently 'badged' using their own terminology. The Strathclyde version runs to about 150 pages and like all Scottish forces is part of the FOI Publication Scheme.[4] The introduction to this document establishes its aims:

Use of the Retention and Management Schedule will:

- Identify those records worth preserving
- Prevent premature destruction of records
- Prevent unnecessary retention of records
- Promote a consistent approach to record keeping where there are no statutory requirements
- Contribute to the Force records management programme
- Promote public confidence and understanding in records held by Strathclyde Police

The very first two aims of the retention schedule focus on the need to identify records worth preserving and make sure that they are retained. The schedule stops records being destroyed because it attributes a value to information, often before it is even created. Hopefully this will ensure that historical records which are being produced today will survive to accurately reflect the work of the Force: an essential consideration when dealing with electronic records. The aim of the retention schedule is not to shred everything or hide evidence as some detractors may suggest. That would be counter-productive and would work against Force goals. Our information is first and foremost used to run the Force and provide police services. The organisation cannot operate without it. Of course there are backlogs of records being destroyed, but these should have been destroyed years ago and are more of a reflection on the advice available to the force in the past. To illustrate, a sample of a list of records destroyed in 2001 is shown below.

Record	Year
Chief Constable Invitations Accepted	1985
Chief Constable Invitations Accepted	1986
Chief Constable Invitations Declined	1985
Chief Constable Invitations Declined	1986
Chief Constable's Diaries	1990
Chief Constable's Personal Correspondence	1985
Chief Constable's Personal Correspondence	1986
Chief Constable's Visit to L Division	1994

Chief Constable's Visit to L Division	1996
Christmas Buffet	1991
Christmas Buffet Supper Menu/Organisation	1978
Christmas Buffet Supper Menu/Organisation	1981
Christmas Buffet Supper Menu/Organisation	1982
Christmas Buffet Supper Menu/Organisation	1983
Conference Papers. INTERPOL Accra, Ghana	1976
Conference Papers. INTERPOL Manila	1980
Conference Papers. INTERPOL Nairobi	1979
Conference Papers. INTERPOL Panama City	1978
Conference Papers. INTERPOL Stockholm	1977

The previous retention schedule was not up-to-date, was not comprehensive and in fact did not make provision for historical records. Minutes of all meetings, for example, were only to be retained for six years. The new schedule is intended to provide the information staff need to make appropriate decisions about the information they manage.

The volume of records that 10,000 staff produces requires us to set rules, produce guidance and ensure that we have good, accurate, clear searchable information. The retention schedule has three basic instructions: 'retain as an archive', 'destroy after x years' or 'review after x years'. In Strathclyde, records marked 'review' are assessed and weeded by those most familiar with the information and functions first. Thereafter, the records manager makes an assessment and finally the local authority archivist will decide what will be accepted into the repository. (This does not preclude the Force from retaining records it believes to be of historical value that the local authority archives have rejected). This may be considered a dangerous method, but in fact staff think that far more of their information is historically valuable than is actually the case and tend to be over cautious in what they destroy when given the option to review. Guidance on how to review records is included in the Force record retention document.

We are developing new policies and procedures to guarantee intellectual control, including simplifying access, managing security and introducing properly for the first time concepts such as metadata and version control. In addition a new file plan will be introduced to the Force during 2004 to make it easier to find and manage information. Good intellectual controls can be successfully transferred into finding aids for historical records and we now provide the City Council Archives with an electronic inventory of all records transferred as standard. This has involved the individual listing of several thousand personnel files dating from the 1960s to 1985 and creating electronic indexes for special constabulary and war reserve personnel cards that have previously been inaccessible. Having records management as a core function within the Force has allowed resources to be used to carry out this work and perhaps more importantly, responsibility for historical records sits with records management, a policy that in itself is possibly the single biggest advantage to historical records.

The Force has also been investigating its approach to the physical management and preservation of records and information. As previously mentioned, a high percentage of records are now electronic, however it is not feasible at this time to transfer records to the City Archives in this format. While we continue to evaluate research and development in this area, our plan is to microfilm records to ensure permanent preservation. In the past we have microfilmed records in a haphazard way, but this will be more structured in the future. To accommodate electronic records, we will be investigating the use of digital transfer to microfilm. It may be the case that this policy changes as electronic technology improves, but until such time as we can receive proven guarantees about the longevity of electronic storage and modern paper, ink and printing techniques, we see this as the most practical option. Manual records, including photographs, will continue be considered for transfer to the Archives. We have found some rare and interesting film and video footage and have been investigating the possibility of transferring such records to specialist repositories such as the Scottish Film Archives, which again have the appropriate expertise to preserve, organise and facilitate access. Combining our intellectual management and destruction policies, we are able to direct limited resources to the appropriate records rather than wasting money preserving unnecessary information, securing their future physically and intellectually.

The introduction of good records management policies into police forces will have and is already having a positive effect on historical records. Most Scottish forces have recognised that the needs of historical records (and their users) in terms of preservation are best served by a local archive office rather than trying to offer a similar function internally with inappropriate storage and insufficient resources. Budgets do not generally stretch to BS5454 compliant storage, dedicated and qualified archivists and the search room facilities that would be needed. The purpose of the Force is to provide a full range of policing services and in-house management of archives cannot generally be considered an essential function when such good alternatives are available. Strathclyde now has a deposit agreement with our local archives that demands certain standards of care and management for our records. Force staff are beginning to realise the practical value of good historical records and as a result appreciate that they need to be managed properly. Recently we have used our historical records to investigate crimes, develop new equipment and plan operations.

Records management is 40% policy and 60% sales. In other words, policies are the essential foundations on which records management is built, but the real challenge is to make sure that they are carried out. After all, there is little point in developing a retention schedule that identifies and values historical records but is universally ignored and records are destroyed because staff are ignorant of their contents. Records management policies can be formulated to incorporate the needs of historical records past, present and future. But to think that they will do that simply by existing is unrealistic. The real challenge is to put policies into practice, used every day as an intrinsic part of force business and operations, so inherent in everyday work that they are unworthy of comment. Only then will the policies be truly successful and the future of all records be secured. Until then we are only part of the way there.

Notes
1. Police Forces in England/Wales may have appointed professional records managers prior to 2000.
2. Trials are underway to evaluate electronic alternatives in several forces throughout the UK.
3. The summary table from the ACPOS MAP is included as Appendix A.
4. Strathclyde Police Record Retention Schedule is available at www.strathclyde.police.uk
   G:\Records Management\Police Archives\Archive Projects and Talks\Policing Conference Lecture Text.doc

Appendix 1
(Taken from the ACPOS Model Action Plan for Records Management)

Steps Required to Achieve Compliance with the Code of Practice on Records Management. The chronology is based on the FOI Act coming into force on 31 December 2005.

Description	*Code of Practice X-Ref*	*Timescales*
Initial Preparation, Structure and Organisation		
Review current records and information management practice & resources		By 30/06/03
Allocate executive responsibility for records management at Force Executive level and ensure that all information functions are part of the same command team or that there are close working relationships and clear lines of communication and demarcation of duties between them	4.1 5.1	By 30/06/03
Appoint a professionally qualified records manager who will have responsibility for directing the action plan	5.1 5.2	By 30/06/03
Strategy and Resources		
Carry out an information survey and functional analysis in preparation for developing a policy and strategy	6.1 7 8.4	By 30/09/04

Prepare and agree at Policy Group a records management policy	7	By 31/12/03
Prepare a detailed strategic plan for implementing the records management policy		By 31/12/03
Allocate adequate resources to support records management	5.2 5.3	By 31/12/03

Detailed Records Management Procedures

Produce a retention/disposal and management schedule authorised by senior management	9.1 9.5 9.6 9.8	By 31/03/04
Establish an appraisal system/criteria for records with a retention of 'review'	9.4 9.5 9.8	By 31/03/04
Ensure that procedures are in place that enables the quick and efficient location and retrieval of information and to document access, editing and processing	8.3 8.6 8.7	By 31/12/03
Ensure the force business recovery/ disaster plan makes provision for records	6.1 8.9	By 31/12/04
Establish transfer/access arrangements with local archive offices for historical records	9.7 Part 3	By 31/12/04

Training and Information Provision

Establish a competency framework to identify skills and knowledge required by staff and provide appropriate training and development opportunities	5.3	By 31/12/03
Provide a range of guidance and procedure notes and raise awareness of records management issues	5.1 5.3 7.1	Ongoing By 31/12/03

Monitoring and Review

Establish performance management scheme	7.2	By 30/09/04
Review records management policy and procedures regularly	7.3	Ongoing

New Technology

Develop a detailed specification and strategy for the purchase and implementation of an EDRMS and related technology such as workflow and correspondence tracking	8.3 8.5 8.6 8.7 9.2	By 31/12/03 Or in accordance with budgetary provision

International Association of Women Police
P.O. BOX 15207
WEDGWOOD STATION
SEATTLE, WASHINGTON 98115

Jan 28/86

Executive Director
BERYL THOMPSON
Seattle, Washington

OFFICERS

President
CAROL-ANN HALLIDAY
West Vancouver, B.C., Canada

1st Vice-President
JANET CRUMLEY
Chattanooga, Tennessee

2nd Vice-President
MARY DUMAS
Amherst, Massachusetts

3rd Vice-President
KATHLEEN BURKE
New York City, New York

Recording Secretary
MYRA HARMON
Seattle, Washington

Financial Secretary
BRUCE STICKLEY
South Bend, Indiana

Sergeant-at-Arms
DOLORES MOST
Totowa, New Jersey

Historian
KIM ADAMSON
Salt Lake City, Utah

Chaplain
PAM STANLEY
West Palm Beach, Florida

PAST PRESIDENTS

MARY WAMSLEY
Denver, Colorado

CAROLEN BAILEY
St. Paul, Minnesota

ROSIE MASON
Kansas City, Missouri

FELICIA SHPRITZER
New York City, New York

MARY RITA OSTRANDER
Madison, Wisconsin

Editor, Bulletin
ARLETTA VANCE STICKLEY
South Bend, Indiana

Dear Mrs. Parker

    The International Association of Women Police is an international organization dedicated toward professionalism in law enforcement through education and training, encouraging the highest ethical standards, and securing merited recognition of women law enforcement officers and their work. The I.A.W.P. annual training seminar offers excellent training on a wide variety of law enforcement subjects.

    The I.A.W.P. is pleased to announce a scholarship award for a woman law enforcement officer employed outside North America, which will pay expenses to attend the I.A.W.P. Annual Training Seminar to be held September, 1986 in Denver, Colorado.

    The Award is intended to encourage participation by those from countries outside of the United States and Canada and to increase understanding of the roles of women officers in various countries. The officer selected to attend will be asked to give a short presentation related to her job and country.

    If you know of anyone eligible who is interested in the scholarship award, we will welcome applications. Letters of applications for the scholarship should include background and qualifications of the candidate, any specific motivation for attending, and any other relevant information. All applications must be received by JUNE 1, 1986. Please send letters and/or questions to: Lt. Carolen Bailey, St. Paul Police Dept., 101 E. Tenth Street, St. Paul, Minnesota, U.S.A. 55101.

    Attached are objectives and criteria for selection of the International Scholarship Award. Thank you for your assistance

Sincerely,

A letter to the Association of Chief Police Officers from the International Association of Women Police Officers, 1986

Addresses of Relevant Organisations

On publication, at least, the world wide web addresses given here ought to be current. But since the electronic world is still highly mutable, this state of affairs is unlikely to last many years, so I have given postal contact addresses as well, whenever they are available. This list does not pretend to be comprehensive, thus it covers only those institutions which were represented via presentations or exhibitions at the June 2004 conference.

European Centre for the Study of Policing
This is now one of the components of the Open University's International Centre for Comparative Criminological Research. It holds regular seminars on the history of police and crime, and among other activities, maintains an on-line bibliography of British police history, available via its website.
    http://www.open.ac.uk/icccr/
European Centre for the Study of Policing, Department of History, The Open University, Walton Hall, Milton Keynes, MK7 6AA

Police History Society
The UK-based body for all those interested in the study of police history. It has over three hundred members, and issues regular newsletters and a journal.
    http://www.policehistorysociety.co.uk/
Hon. Secretary, 64 Nore Marsh Road, Wootton Bassett, Wiltshire, SN4 8BH

Police Vehicle Enthusiasts' Club
This group has existed since the 1960s. It holds regular events and issues a magazine. As well as collecting old police vehicles, many of its members are also interested in photographs of them.
    http://www.pvec.co.uk/
PVEC, Summer Isles Cottage, Bagpath, Tetbury, Gloucestershire, GL8 8YG

International Police Association
Both the international administrative centre and the headquarters of the British branch of this independent association are located in Nottingham. The IPA has published the comprehensive guide to Police and Crime Museums of the World.
    http://www.ipa-iac.org
International Police Association, International Administration Centre, 1 Fox Road, West Bridgford, Nottingham, NG2 6AJ

Liverpool University Centre for Archive Studies
This research and teaching centre is at the forefront of critical and developmental engagement with archivists and the users of archives.
    http://www.liv.ac.uk/lucas/
LUCAS, School of History, University of Liverpool, 9 Abercromby Square, Liverpool, L69 3BX

West Midlands Police Museum
The West Midlands Police Museum houses a wide range of pictures, information and items to show the development of policing in and around Birmingham.
    http://www.westmidlandspolicemuseum.co.uk/
Sparkhill Police Station, 639 Stratford Road, Sparkhill, Birmingham, B11 4EA

Essex Police Museum
Established in 1991 to advance the education of the public in the history of Essex in general and in the Essex Police Service in particular', it holds archival material relating to the history of the force from 1840, including personnel, disciplinary and other records, together with more general documents and a large photographic record.

Addresses of Relevant Organisations 153

http://www.essex.police.uk/pages/offbeat/o_bt_mus.htm
Essex Police Headquarters, PO Box 2, Springfield, Chelmsford, Essex, CM2 6DA

Belfast Police Museum
This was set up in 1983 to record the history of the RIC and the RUC in Northern Ireland, and it continues to perform this function for the Police Service of Northern Ireland.
http://www.psni.police.uk/index/pg_police_museum/
The Police Museum, Police Service of Northern Ireland, Headquarters, Brooklyn, 65 Knock Road, Belfast, BT5 6LE

South East Museums Libraries and Archives Council
This is the regional development agency for the museum, library and archive sector in the South East.
http://www.semlac.org.uk/
SEMLAC, 15 City Business Centre, Hyde Street, Winchester, Hants, SO23 7TA

National Archives
This body maintains the central archive of government records at the Public Record Office in Kew. It also has a remit to 'advise government departments and the wider public sector on best practice in records management'.
http://www.nationalarchives.gov.uk/
The National Archives, Kew, Richmond, Surrey, TW9 4DU

Crime, Histoire et Sociétés/Crime, History and Societies
This bilingual (English and French) journal deals with all aspects of criminal justice history. It is published in conjunction with the International Association for the History of Crime and Criminal Justice.
http://www.droz.org/biblioeng/chs-en.html
Crime, history & societies, René Lévy, Cesdip, Immeuble Edison, 43, Boulevard Vauban, F- 78280 Guyancourt, France

Galleries of Justice
This is Nottingham's award-winning museum, whose collections cover all aspects of criminal and civil justice.
   http://www.galleriesofjustice.org.uk/
Shire Hall, High Pavement, Lace Market, Nottingham, NG1 1HN

The Yorkshire Law and Order Museums
These three linked and complementary museums in Ripon – the Prison & Police Museum, the Workhouse Museum, and the Courthouse Museum – are all managed by the Ripon Museum Trust.
   http://www.riponmuseums.co.uk/
Yorkshire Law and Order Museums, 27 St Marygate, Ripon, North Yorkshire, HG4 1LX

Epping Forest District Museum
Among much other material, this houses the local Waltham Abbey Police Historical Collection.
   http://www.eppingforestdistrictmuseum.co.uk/
Epping Forest District Museum, 39-41 Sun Street, Waltham Abbey, Essex, EN9 1EL

Museums, Libraries and Archives Council
National government body with responsibility for this sector.
   http://www.mla.gov.uk